The best of
YOU

*How to unlock your own
unique potential*

Mark Brown

The Best of You
How to unlock your own unique potential

Copyright © 2021 Mark Brown

ISBN:

978-1-80227-173-7 (Hardback)
978-1-80227-105-8 (Paperback)
978-1-80227-106-5 (eBook)

This book is dedicated to my wife Laura, and to my children Kristopher, Joshua and Olivia. Thank you for continually bringing out the Best in Me.

Table of Contents

Introduction

Having recently tried to declutter my ever-growing collection of books, I noticed that over 50% of these books would be under the genre of self-help and personal development.

The self-help industry has boomed over the last 2 decades with a Google search offering literally hundreds of thousands of books that aim to help with anything from anxiety to weight loss, from meditation and mindfulness to unleashing the warrior within.

This book aims to strip back and simplify some of the key areas of self-care and look at some of the real-life skills and tools that can help us truly take control of our own future starting right here and now, as we embark on the greatest journey of all to find the Best of You.

My own self-help journey started when I was 12 years old, and, after a 3-week hospitalisation, being diagnosed with the autoimmune disease, ulcerative colitis.

At the time, I was a self-confessed hypochondriac who couldn't even bear to watch Casualty on a Saturday night for fear of catching some life-threatening illness and couldn't stand the thought of ever spending a night in a hospital due to all the diseases I could catch, therefore, I was ecstatic, to say the least, to be home after my own hospital visit.

That said, I was struggling with the diagnosis of having something that was labelled as chronic and lifelong and would mean many return trips to the hospital over the years and that I would likely need surgery at some point.

As far back as I can remember, my parents had always called me a born worrier. At the time, this was relatively true, in that I did worry about almost everything, and when there was nothing to worry about, I would then worry about not worrying! Sound familiar? But no one is born a worrier; the stories we create and tell ourselves over and over and the stories we are continually told about ourselves ultimately shape our view of our world and ourselves. The good news is we can change our story and our future, we just need to be willing to take charge; this is something we will look more closely at later.

Almost every modern disease, condition and illness in the modern western world can be linked to stress and worry.

My intention in this book is to share with you part of my own journey and how I have learned some key skills and tools which have helped me lead a more content and fulfilling life and to share some insight into the power that each and every one of us holds within in us to take control and positively shape our future.

For the last decade, I have been delivering my award-winning Best of You Programme for schools, colleges, the prison service, social work services and for those who are ready to explore their true potential. Before running my own company, I spent time designing and delivering values-led leadership programmes on the beautiful Isle of Skye, and this followed several years of working in social work and criminal justice services.

Aside from my family, my biggest passion in life is human potential. This book aims to capture some of the journey and stories I have had the privilege to be a part of and introduces you to some of the amazing people I have met along the way who have helped me find the best in me.

Throughout this book, there will be opportunities to pause for reflection and take a little time out to try out some of these simple and highly effective tools and strategies. An important piece of guidance before you embark on this journey is to ensure that you do take the time to try out all that is offered. This book may indeed act as medication or even meditation for the soul, but like everything in life worth doing, it only works if you try it......

CHAPTER 1

The Best of Times

"It was the best of times, it was the worst of times, it was the age of wisdom, it was the age of foolishness"

~ Charles Dickens

I think this still stands true today in 2020. We live in a world where technology is at its most advanced and continues to advance at an incredible rate. We can learn almost anything at the push of a button, we are never more than a day away from any place or anyone in the world, we are more connected to the rest of the world than we have ever been and medical advancements have progressed so much in the last few decades that many conditions which once wiped out generations are now controlled with a simple jab of the needle or some drops for the nose! Heck, as if that's not enough, if you fancy some intergalactic travel, then Richard Branson and Elon Musk are ploughing their own fortunes into making this happen within their own lifetime, so if you want to get off this twirling rock, then things are on the up! So, in many ways, you could say this is, indeed, the Best of Times.

On the other hand, we also live in a world where world leaders taunt each other over social media, launch test missiles over each other's countries and mock and rile each other to the point that another world war feels imminent. It is also impossible to go a day without hearing of some tragedy on the news - a child going missing, another celebrity paedophile or another terror attack somewhere in the world. Our news feeds are riddled with fear-inducing information that is hard to switch off from when programmed on a daily basis. So, you could also say it is, indeed, the worst of times.

One of the things I have learned over the years is that it very much depends on what you are looking for regarding the above perspectives. There is a saying "where your focus goes, energy flows".

I am not saying that if you don't focus on the news or if you delete your Facebook and news apps that these things that cause so much stress and worry won't happen, but we do often concern ourselves and worry about things that sometimes A, never happen, and B, don't directly affect us.

As a child, I know I did this a lot. If I heard that someone was ill, I would worry that I would become ill. If I heard that someone was being bullied, I would worry I might be bullied. My mum was a nurse and devoted her life to looking after the elderly, and occasionally I would hear of someone who was gravely ill which would send my own anxiety into overdrive. I remember leaving the living room at home whenever a hospital programme would come on for fear of hearing about some condition that I might catch. This behaviour was often laughed at and brushed off as "Och, that's just Mark, he is a born worrier, worries about everything". It wasn't entirely helpful, this label of being a born worrier, as it left me feeling a bit isolated and spending a lot of time in my own head. Nowadays, I don't mind spending a lot of time in my own head as I have worked to become one of my own best counsellors, but more on that later.

In regard to our energy and where we choose to focus this, I am not going to get into the details of the law of attraction, as that is a whole story within itself. And although the hugely successful book 'The Secret' by Rhonda Byrne suggests that whatever we think about we attract, there should be a bit of a health warning with this as it works with both the good and the bad thoughts.

I spend most of my time these days working in schools and within projects with both young people and adults who are riddled with stress, anxiety and worry and who are searching for a means to an end to their daily struggles with life and all that has led them to their current situation. The current stats on stress and anxiety within young people are that now more than 50% of young people in school will experience stress or anxiety-related issues within their time at school. I am not saying that this wasn't the case when I was at school; I know for a fact I struggled with stress and anxiety for part of my teen years and some of this was around fitting in at school, was I good enough, what will I do when I leave, what if I don't get the grades, etc., what if I get ill? But now, it is a whole different ball game. With the birth of social media, cyber-bullying, celebrity, smartphones, and above all, standardised testing, there are so many things that young people compare themselves to and are compared to, adding to their constant struggle to maintain their place in modern society with good mental health intact.

A big part of what I teach and share in schools and the other projects that I am involved in is the ability to grow confidence, motivation, inspiration and aspiration. These were not just four things that I plucked at random and designed an award-winning programme for. No, this came from spending about 15 years working with people of all ages and stages and noticing the patterns of behaviours and hearing the same stories of "If only I had been more motivated at school" and "I wish I had had more confidence at school".

If you ask a group of young people, or teachers for that matter, what schools teach, they will likely respond by naming a number of academic subjects, and you might even hear a few responses around responsible citizens and effective contributors. (This is especially the case if you are in Scotland where the curriculum is based around the Curriculum for Excellence). This itself is part of the problem whereby people are graded on their excellence or their lack thereof.

Another part of my life's work over the past 15 years has been to support and help shift a much-needed change of direction within education. At the time of writing the book, I am currently delivering programmes across Scotland in schools, prisons, community projects and charities. The Best of You Programme was born out of my desire and passion to help people explore their own unique potential and uncover what they have yet to become.

Having worked with groups of all ages and stages since my early 20s, one thing I know to be sure, having witnessed it time and time again, is that we all have something to offer this world; a gift, a talent, a skill, a behaviour, a way of being, something that sets us aside from others. Some of us know it at a young age and some don't find it until later in life, but one thing I know for sure is that we all have something unique to offer during our time here.

This is not some throw-away, blindly optimistic compliment to all those with whom I have worked over the years, or some liberal hippy view of the world.

I have had people referred to my programmes through schools, social work, prison services and criminal justice programmes who have been deemed as society write-offs for whatever reason. In the early days of the programmes, they often present with a sort of pseudo bravado which really acts as a bit of a self-preservation tool for them and allows them to hide behind false confidence, and this can also show up in other ways, such as the joker of the group, the bully or the arrogant one. On the other side, they can also show up as painfully shy, anxiety-ridden, full of fear, mute or just disengaged.

The key to working with and not being affected by any of these behaviours is to realise that they are just that, behaviours, and behaviours always show up for a reason. Behaviours often come from emotions, and emotions always have a stimulus, therefore something usually happens or has happened which will influence participants' behaviour on a programme. Understanding this and being ok with this are key to building an honest and authentic rapport with the group.

The most important thing on my agenda for every single programme is to have a real connection with each person on the programme; this is when you know you can have an impact – when the masks come off and the behaviours subside, and you have what can sometimes just be a moment of real authenticity with someone and you see and feel a real sense of potential for them and, even more importantly, they feel it and see it for themselves. Often, it takes a few days, sometimes even the whole week of a programme for this to happen, but the feeling you get when it does happen? Well, that's why I do what I do.

A Young Offender

A few years ago, I was working up on the Isle of Lewis in the Outer Hebrides of Scotland. I was running a Best of You Programme for a group of young men who had fallen into the criminal justice system and one of the young men who had been nominated for the programme came with a whole lot of reputation behind him. He was known as a volatile drug addict with a drink problem and a criminal background, having spent much of his adult life in various Scottish prisons. On day one of the programme, he was easily the most challenging in the group and I could see the impact he was having on the rest of the group. He knew his reputation alone was enough to have many of the other members fear him and he knew that his background almost gave permission for him to be top dog in this group. He challenged almost everything I said and tried hard to dominate the conversations in the group by sharing some of his stories of being in prison. He often looked to me for a reaction when he would share a short story of his prison life. "I mind one time I was in Barlinnie, and some cunt nicked ma Custard Creams fae ma cell; well, I had no choice but to slash the cunt's cheek when I found out who it wiz!" then he would stare at me to check my response.

These stories would show up throughout the week as he tried to maintain his place of dominance in the group and my lack of reaction to the stories seemed to help them lessen as the days went on. On meeting him on day one, I made a choice, as I have done with so many others over the years, that I would not judge him on his past and what brought him here, but focus more on where he is right now in front of me each day and what he could yet become. For me, that is the real key to building any purposeful relationship. When someone shows up and they appear to not yet be at their best or they are stuck in their past and portray what I mentioned earlier as a sort of pseudo bravado, you have 2 options: One, you can try and challenge them to alter their behaviour through offering support or challenge or even punishment, depending in which establishment you are working in, or two, you can accept them as they are, for now, knowing that their behaviour has more than likely come from some sort of trauma or tough reality experience which has resulted in the behaviours you are presented with. You also have the pleasure of helping them become the best version of themselves by creating an environment that is safe to explore and learn in.

This lad from Lewis rebelled to almost everything I was offering and, at the end of day 3 of the programme, waited to the end of the session and until everyone had left and asked me why I hadn't yet thrown him off the programme. "I haven't thrown anyone off a programme since I started this 7 years ago," I said.

"But do you not think I am being disruptive and a bit of an arse?" "Well, yeah, but you clearly know that, so there's no point in me telling you something you already know, now is there?"

"Ach, I'm only here to get my community service hours down anyway, pal, so I'm not really bothered either way."

"Ok, I'll do you a deal. I will sort it with your parole officer that you will get the hours for this week back regardless of whether you show up or not; how does that sound?"

"Why would you do that? Ah, see! Ye are chucking me off; fuck sake, told ye!"

"No, I'm not chucking you off at all, it's just that if you're only here to get your hours back and not really getting anything from it, then there is not much point in being here, given that I will ensure you get your hours back anyway, is there?"

"Aye, that's fine, pal, you do that. What a fucking waste of time the last three days were then, eh?" and off he went.

Now, it's a bit of a gamble to take this line with people on the programme who are often disruptive. One of two things will happen; you will either never hear from them again and they will take you up on it, or they will show up the next day and want to see the week through regardless of community service hours.

And lo and behold, the next day this lad showed up, early! I asked him why he decided to come back on day 4 and he said, "Well, there's only 2 more days, eh? Would be as well just to finish it and get the certificate at the end, eh?"

On this day, there was a shift in his behaviour. I noticed him focus more, interrupt less and actually noticed some leadership during the challenges.

Again, at the end of the day, he waited behind until everyone was leaving and I was tidying up and he started to help to put the chairs away as another group was coming in to do yoga afterwards.

"Can I ask you a question?" he said.

"Aye, go for it."

"Why do you do what you do? Ah mean, why are you the way you are with us?"

"What do you mean?" I asked.

"Well, it doesn't seem to matter how mental we get, or hyper or like abusive to you or each other, you just stay dead calm, have a bit of banter with us and then you like just like tell us a wee story and we all start behaving good again and just get on with it. Why are you like that?" (It was never as simple as that, but I got his point).

What a brilliant question!! I didn't say that out loud, but I thought it in my head. I also thought what an insightful question to ask when, only 24 hours ago, he was telling me that he was only there for the community service hours.

"Well, you see, my experience of school wasn't great. I wasn't the smartest in the class, nor the dumbest, but I can tell you that I hated when a teacher shouted at me, or anyone else for that matter. I hated teachers being sarcastic and couldn't stand seeing people being made a fool of or someone thinking they were better than them.

"I had one teacher, and his gift to this world was that he was a great listener. If a pupil stepped out of line, he would invite them up to his desk and not demand, he would tell the others to get on with their work and he would sit with that person and just listen to what was going on for them. More often than not, the pupil just needed a little space and a little time and some attention with someone to listen and at least act like they cared. At the opposite side of this, I had other teachers that would scream at you and make you stand up in front of the class and belittle and verbally abuse you with a view that the embarrassment would be deterrent enough for it not to happen again. Guess what teacher had the best relationships and the best results?"

"Aye, but this isn't school and you're no' a teacher; none of us need to even be here!"

"Exactly. I see everywhere as a sort of classroom. In every situation, there is an opportunity to learn; the trick is to create the right conditions and to create an environment that people want to be in so that they can explore their potential and ultimately not be judged for what they have done, but for what they can actually still become."

He didn't say much after that, but as he left, he said, "Thanks, see you the morra."

No sarcasm, no abuse, just a genuine thank you and a show of acknowledgement and appreciation.

Throughout every single programme I run, I write about every participant at the end of the sessions - just a few lines of what I have noticed and appreciated that day. On the final night of the programme, I put this all together in the form of a personalised graduation script. I read this out to them at their graduation on the last day of the programme by way of sharing my appreciation of them taking the time to commit to the programme and commit to exploring their own unique potential. This is read out to them in front of their peers and any guests who may be at the ceremony.

This can often be a very personal and emotional moment on the programme for the individuals, and for many, it is the first time they have ever heard anything good about themselves. However, it also can be a catalyst for participants to start making the changes that they need to be more in control of their future and to begin exploring the habits and putting into practice what they have learned on the programme.

So, one thing that I know is true, having spent almost 20 years working with a range of diverse groups of all ages, is that when the right conditions are created, the right questions asked and the right stories shared, profound and lasting change is absolutely possible.

I also know that as a parent, one of the golden rules I stick by is "monkey see, monkey do" so I know that almost all the behaviours that I show and words that I choose on a daily basis are picked up by my children and will undoubtedly be mirrored back to me regardless of it being good or bad. I also adopt the "monkey see, monkey do" attitude on programmes, whether in schools or working with offenders; I choose to be mindful of my words, my tone and my reactions. Teachers often ask me how I manage to control students and groups that they often struggle with, and the truth is, I don't control them, I control myself. I am always sure of what I am saying and if people try to talk over me or if I notice them speaking when I am, I gently draw attention to it, without raising my voice or showing that it has had any effect on me and tell them, "I will just wait until you're ready". They often stop immediately as the unintended pressure of everyone now looking at them is enough for them to stop, but the tone and non-threatening words are key to the situation being resolved without being escalated. Once you have done this a few times within the group, a habit is quickly created and learned, and levels of respect within the group start to form.

You will often find that shouty teachers have shouty pupils and calm and quiet teachers have calm and quiet pupils. Teachers, lecturers and facilitators alike always have the power to set the tone in the room. High levels of self-awareness of the words, tone and volume in how you speak play a huge part in setting the right tone to create the right atmosphere.

To help set the tone around personal change and how to begin the process, I often ask participants on the first day of a programme to think about and discuss the 2 questions below.

1. Exploring change

1. If you could change something about yourself right now in the here and now, not something from your past, or something that you have no control over, but something that you could actually make a decision to change about your life, what might that be?

   I encourage them to think about what this might feel like, what they would notice about themselves and what impact it may have on them.

2. What would you need to find within yourself to allow that change to begin?

I would like you to take a few moments to answer these 2 questions for yourself. Put the book down just for a few moments and think about what you might choose to change about yourself in the here and now, because you know if you made this change and it became part of who you are and what you're capable of becoming, it would massively impact the rest of your life. Then, think about what you feel you would need to find more of within yourself to allow the change to happen.

Having asked these 2 questions literally hundreds of times, to hundreds of people, I have noticed and collected a cluster and theme of similar answers to question 2. Yours may be here too, but it is fine if it isn't.

Confidence
Motivation
Energy
Forgiveness
Willpower
Discipline
Hope
Self-Belief
Strength
Inner peace

What I love about hearing these responses is that they are very real, very possible and completely accessible, but as I said, the conditions need to be right. And in this case, it's the conditions that you create in your own head and, indeed, in your own life that will be the difference between whether this becomes a reality for you or not.

You may or may not be the kind of person who spends a lot of time thinking about reflective questions like the two above, but just giving yourself the time to think about them, reflect on them, recognise them and then either say them out loud or write them down, brings them closer to the front of your mind and begins the process of uncovering what is needed to make these changes possible.

We are both conditioned and programmed to believe that our minds and our behaviours are hard-wired. I was brought up in an era of a fixed mindset of "What's for ye won't go by ye", loosely meaning what will be will be. I fought against this from an early age as it sounded so mundane and predictable. I also had to fight against this when, at the age of 12 years old, I became very ill and was hospitalised with the autoimmune condition ulcerative colitis. I remember after diagnosis, the consultant telling my mum and me that I would likely need a number of surgeries throughout my life to keep the condition under control and that this would be a life-altering condition and would ultimately have a significant impact on my life.

Only part of the above was true. For a while, this condition did play a significant part in my life and I did spend many years with long and painful flare-ups and was put on a cocktail of drugs to try and keep the symptoms at bay. However, I sit here in my office at home, a week away from 41 years old, having never needed surgery (reaches for a bit of wood to touch) and never even taken a day off work due to this condition.

This was not due to some super drug or that I was just lucky and the condition never really took hold of me. Believe me, in the early days, it really did take hold. No, this is largely down to 4 things:

1. At age 16, I started researching self-healing and alternative healing and have continued this throughout my life.

2. This one took the longest - I stopped overreacting to the condition and didn't react to every little symptom. Our physical bodies tend to take their lead from our thoughts, regardless of whether these thoughts are real or not. So, I spent a lot of time practising the art of non-reaction (See chapter 5).

3. I learned both meditation and Reiki as forms of self-healing. Meditation for me is not really about inner peace or calming the mind, it is about realising that not all thoughts are real, therefore we don't always need to act on them.

4. I try to walk somewhere every single day for at least 40 minutes. Our bodies respond well to movement, and our minds tend to be a bit more under control when we are outside and in nature, or even just outside our homes walking without a particular destination in mind. I have walked away about

80% of my worries over the years and, as the Native Americans say, "a man's best doctors are his legs"!

Regarding the belief that our mind and behaviours are hard-wired, we don't need to look too far to find evidence that this just isn't true.

I have worked in the field of human addictions for almost 20 years, in communities, in prisons and in schools. I have seen addicts with a heroin addiction of 20 years + only to finally kick it and move on with their lives, and alcoholics who do eventually have their final drink then take control and go on to live sober and purposeful lives, and it's not rare! I have seen this countless times over the years.

I remember watching Russell Brand many years ago when he was the presenter on Big Brother, and at the time, I remember thinking what an arrogant egotistical arsehole of a man. His behaviour and demeanour were ones that I found disgusting. He later revealed that during this time, he was actively using heroin amongst other class A drugs. Now, on watching him all these years ago, in the public eye, winning Shagger of the Year award and living a life of drink, drugs, celebrity and media whore, you might think one of two things; he will either be another A list celeb who burns out too quickly, or he will make some career-ending mistake that brings him out of the public eye for good. Both almost happened. Now, if you were to take a few minutes and look at Russell Brand's online presence, including his social media and published work over the past few years, you would be presented with a completely different human being than before. Russell's focus, identity, reputation and purpose are now one of sobriety, a campaigner for social justice, spirituality, a leader of public thought and a passionate activist for mental health and drug rehabilitation.

The subject of behaviours not being so hard-wired also brings to mind the legendary guitarist, Eric Clapton. Through the late '60s, all of the '70s and the 80s, Clapton may have been turning out timeless classics like Layla and Wonderful Tonight, but behind the scenes, Clapton was a chronic drug addict and battled both drink and drugs for over 2 decades before finally getting clean. Again, fast forward to the present day and Clapton is still regarded as one of the most influential guitarists of all time, however, he is now sober, clean of all drugs and runs Crossroads, his addiction treatment centre in Antigua.

Now, these are both just snapshots of two people who have been in the public eye for many years, so it is fairly easy to research their story, but having met and worked with literally thousands of people over the years who have chosen to put the work into rewiring their thought patterns, I have first-hand evidence that rewiring and reprogramming your mind is 100% possible when you know how and put the work in.

> *"Imagination is everything, it's a preview of life's coming attractions"*
> ~ **Albert Einstein**

I love this quote by Einstein. These 10 words probably changed my whole outlook on life when I was about 14 years old and, then again, in later life. The words we choose to listen to and the words we choose to share in any given moment can have a massive impact on every area of our lives, but more on that later.

I met my first shaman when I was 14 years old. I had already had 2 or 3 years of taking all sorts of drugs to try and suppress the often painful and debilitating symptoms of ulcerative colitis, but nothing was really keeping the condition under control. My gran, who was a huge influence on my life, and still is, had introduced me to a woman who was a reiki practitioner. I didn't know much about it at the time, only that my gran had regular treatments to help her own condition of lymphatic leukaemia. My gran told me that this was a non-invasive therapy and was a form of energy healing and that it could help with symptoms, pain and my anxiety over having the condition. I remember asking my gran what would happen during the treatment, as I had had many treatments and exploratory procedures at the hospital over the years, cameras going up here, there and everywhere, liquids going in and out and up and down - you get the picture. But when my gran said, "Don't worry, she won't even touch you", I have to be honest, I was less than hopeful that this would have any sort of impact on what was now becoming a progressively worse condition and taking over my daily life. I had already missed months of school over the last few years and there was already talk of me repeating a year which filled me full of even more anxiety and worry, so, in the end, I decided to give this reiki thing a try.

My first session was on a Sunday morning. I would love to be one of those people who could say it was a cold Sunday morning in July 1993 at around 11 am. Truth be told, I am not really one for detail, but I know it was a Sunday because I went right after watching Glen Michael's Cartoon Cavalcade with Paladin, the talking lamp!

The woman was based and worked out of a wee cottage in Edinburgh. My gran drove me to the cottage and introduced me to Kate, who would be giving me the treatment. I remember Kate answering the door and, as I recall, she was a very large woman who filled the doorway. She had a huge smile on her face, was very pleased to see my gran (most people were) and she was wearing this very long, very colourful dress. I wasn't in the best mood as I was nervous, and I remember thinking to myself, "Jeez, she's dressed like a fucking lava lamp," but in I went to see what it was all about.

Before she started, Kate told me that she would not need to lay a hand on me for the duration of the session and that all I had to do was lie back and relax. About 10 minutes into the treatment, I opened my eyes with a bit of a jolt and said, "You said you wouldn't touch me!" To my surprise, when I opened my eyes, Kate's hands were about 6 inches above my stomach, but I could feel something going on inside, like a pressure lifting and shifting. She told me just to lie back, close my eyes and let her work on some energy that needed shifting.

About an hour later, she had finished, and I opened my eyes, lying there on the treatment table. Kate brought me a glass of water and told me to drink it then join her in the living room when I was ready.

A few minutes later, I went in and Kate was sitting on the couch and asked me to have a seat. She asked how I was feeling. This was hard to describe as I felt somewhere in between just about to fall asleep and just waking up, but one thing that was noticeable was that for the first time in ages, my mind wasn't racing and overthinking every thought. I also noticed that my stomach did not have the usual knot in it which felt like having stomach cramp 24 hours a day. In short, I told Kate that I definitely felt better than when I went in and I thanked her for the treatment. Kate told me that she believed that something that might help my condition would be to learn to view it differently and to learn to relax, calm my mind and begin to worry less about what may or may not happen. She was probably the first person to teach me that the physical body really does take its lead from the metaphysical mind. Although I was too young to understand it at the time, it wasn't long before I began to experiment with this and started to notice changes. Before I left that day after my first reiki experience, Kate gave me some home practice, which was to spend a little time each day imagining what a healthy colon on the inside and out would look and feel like. She asked that I take just 10-15 minutes a day when I was in a position to relax and visualise the inside of my gut literally healing itself of all inflammation and toxins. Like everything in life, when we put the work in and practise things, we get good at it, and when we get good at things, they have an impact.

It wasn't long before I was making this visualisation technique part of my morning and evening practice and although symptoms were still persisting, I was genuinely starting to feel better inside my own head.

I went for reiki treatments about once a month and started to get to know Kate really well and she began to teach me a lot about the power of the human spirit, our ability to heal and the importance of what we spend time thinking about. A few months after our first session, I had an appointment at the hospital as I was due for another horrid colonoscopy; this was one of the procedures that I dreaded the most due to the preparation, the discomfort and ultimately, what they might find. An hour or so after the procedure, I was invited in to speak with my consultant who had the results of the colonoscopy. I remember being a little drowsy after the sedation, but I do remember him asking how I had been feeling and what had I been doing that was different than before. I asked what he meant, and he brought out pictures of the results that I'd had done a few months previously. The scope from a few months ago highlighted about 60% severe inflammation in my lower bowel, where today's scope showed only 15% mild inflammation. The consultant (Dr Holden) seemed both impressed and puzzled by the results. He shared that he did not expect anywhere near this level of improvement in such a short time and that he could not remember a time in his career where he had seen such a reduction in inflammation. He asked what I had been doing or if I had been taking anything different over the past few months. I sheepishly looked at him and told him the only thing I was doing differently was going for regular reiki sessions and working on my own levels of worry through learning to meditate and trying to visualize a healthier internal gut. I remember him saying something along the lines of "Whatever works for you" and "There is no scientific proof to suggest that reiki works at all" (25 years later and there is a shit load of scientific evidence that proves the impact the energy healing has).

If I fast forward to a year or two later, I remember sitting in the very same chair with the very same consultant and having just been for another fairly successful scope. I knew my doctor fairly well at this point as he had been my consultant for a few years. At the end of the consultation, he said, "By the way, are you still getting your (and then he put his fingers up inverted comma style) "reiki" done?" This riled me a bit at the time as he was mocking the therapy that, for me, was clearly having a huge healing impact, along with the other work I was practising on my mindset. I asked him, "Why don't you believe that me having this energy therapy on a regular basis is having a positive impact on my gut healing?" His response was, "Look, Mark, I have been a consultant and surgeon for over 20 years; in all the bodies that I have opened and operated on, I can honestly say I have never experienced, seen or witnessed anything that resembles a chakra, meridian or healing light - it's just not there. What you're potentially experiencing is the placebo effect, nothing more."

Placebo or not, I couldn't give a flying fuck. I was getting better and my mind was helping steer my gut to better health. Before I left the consultation room that day, I asked the doctor who was in the picture at the side of his computer. It was of a woman in her late 40s and two younger girls in their teens. I had seen the picture many times over the years but had never asked. "My wife and daughters," he replied, "why?" "I was feeling a mixture of bravery and frustration at his despondency around my belief and work around self-healing, so I asked him, "Do you love them?" "Of course, I do!" he almost snapped his response, and it had a slightly higher tone at the end as if to say what a stupid question.

"How do you know?" I asked.

"How do I know what?"

"That you love them?"

"I don't see what this has to do with your consultation, Mark. Just keep doing what you're doing, and I will see you in a few months."

"Can I ask you one more question before I go, Doctor?"

"If you must."

"If you were to go for surgery this afternoon and the surgeon were to open YOU up, would he find love and proof that you love your wife and daughters" Silence....

"That's completely different, Mark. See you in a few months."

I was not trying to be a cheeky 16-year-old or indeed to mock him, but I was trying to explore the idea that just because you can't see or feel something, doesn't mean it doesn't exist!

Back then, I probably spent about an hour spread throughout the day thinking about, visualising and imagining a healthy version of myself, one that didn't worry as much and one that didn't react and worry about every little symptom that showed up as this played a huge part in how my body would respond. Einstein's quote about imagination, to me, is more relevant today than ever before. If we allow ourselves the time and space to imagine what yet might be possible for us and what changes we have the power to make, then the only difference between success and failure is the ability to act on our imagination. And how do we do this? By getting the "stuff" out of our heads and into reality.

We know this is possible as we have centuries of evidence of people turning their ideas and imaginations into life-changing reality. YOU are no different.

Here are some examples below of how people tuned into their imagination and took action and turned it into a reality.

Roger Bannister – **Imagination** – I can run a mile in 4 minutes. No one has done it before – **Action** – train hard, believe you can do it, don't give up until it's done – **Result** – In 1954, becomes the first human being to run a mile in under four minutes.

Steve Jobs – **Imagination** – Change the world of communication for the better and keep it simple – **Action** – design the most technologically advanced communication tool that can fit in your pocket – **Result**

— CEO for one of the world's biggest and most successful companies and continues to push the boundaries of technology.

JK Rowling – **Imagination** – Become a writer - "As soon as I knew what writers were, I wanted to be one." – **Action** – One day. on a delayed train from Manchester to London, she starts to write about a little boy called Harry who finds out he is a wizard. – **Result** - Becomes one of the world's most-loved writers, personal wealth of over £600 million after losing her billionaire status due to her incredible philanthropic endeavours.

Blake Mycoskie – **Imagination** - Help people who cannot afford shoes - **Action** – Start a worldwide shoe company, "TOMS", whereby for every pair of TOMS shoes that are purchased, a second pair is provided for those who cannot afford them – **Result** – Millions of people around the world no longer suffer from foot injuries and have shoes to walk in.

Adam Braun – **Imagination** – It began with a question that led to an imagination. I met a small boy begging in the streets of India. "What do you want most in the world?" "A pencil," he replied! – **Action** – Start

Pencils of Promise, a not-for-profit organisation that builds schools and trains teachers in the developing world – **Result** - 524 schools have been built in developing countries with 108,643 students being taught daily.

Now, this is a very small number and just a few examples of a much larger group of people who have tapped into their imagination to lead a life of passion and purpose and ultimately find the best in themselves. Before we move on and explore how we get our ideas out of our heads and into reality, take a few quiet moments, put the book down and allow yourself to ponder this question.

2. Question for success

Imagine success was your only option; what might you do differently with your life?

Write just a few lines of what came up for you.

_____

_____

_____

_____

CHAPTER 2

Out of your Mind

"Curiosity is the engine of achievement"
~ Sir Ken Robinson

After leaving school and spending many years as a full-time musician, playing in blues bands and show bands throughout Scotland, along with a vast array of other jobs to pay the bills, including forklift driver, warehouse worker and produce assistant, to name but a few, I decided in my early 20s to devote my working life to working with and supporting young people and adults from tough and challenging realities. I've been a youth worker, a drugs worker, a throughcare worker (working with young people who are looked after by the authority and not by parents) a programme director for a youth leadership charity and now director of my own company working with young people and adults throughout the UK by delivering my award-winning Best of You Programmes in education establishments, prisons, social work services and criminal justice services.

In 2005, I was working for Falkirk Council as a throughcare worker. My role was to work alongside and support young people in the care system and help them transition into independent living. At this point in my own life, the power of imagination, manifestation and visualisation had already become a firmly rooted habit in my life. So, when working with the young people that were referred to me, I would encourage them to think about their future, to visualise and fantasise about what they could achieve and would yet become. And when they were finally allocated their own houses from the council housing services, I would spend a lot of time getting them to really think about how they wanted their first home to look and feel and I would help them get the images from their imagination into reality. This was one of the more rewarding parts of the job. Towards the end of my time with the council, I was headhunted by a charity delivering values-led leadership programmes on the Isle of Skye. I had taken a few groups on their programmes in the years before and liked what the charity was offering and how they worked with young people from diverse backgrounds. My role was to be Head of Programmes for their YPLA programmes

(Young People Leadership Academy Programmes) and help further develop and implement the programme throughout Scotland. The programme that was already in place at the charity had been designed by a Canadian called Ian Chisholm and was based around 6 core values of Awareness, Focus, Creativity, Integrity, Perseverance and Service (AFCIPS for short). The purpose of the programme was to work with a group of about 12 young people and 3 staff from schools, social work services and other youth services and help them explore their own core values whilst using the framework of AFCIPS as a structure for the week. At the end of the week, if the young people and staff had stuck to the programme and attended all sessions whilst working hard each day, then the programme would conclude with a certified graduation. This was often the most powerful part of the week as the young people would be given offerings of support and appreciation by the programme's delivery team in the form of a graduation script which had been written and created throughout the week by way of celebrating their week and acknowledging what they had achieved and also what they may yet become.

I had 9 great years at this charity, and having spent many years travelling around the UK and driving to the Isle of Skye (a 500-mile round trip) literally hundreds of times, I decided to move on from the organisation; it was not an easy decision to make. During my 9 years there, the charity had seen 5 different CEOs, all with their own style of leadership and all with their own agenda and vision for the charity. The current leadership during my last chapter there did not entirely chime with my own core values and vision for the charity, and although I had thought about it for many months in my mind and had already started to manifest and visualise what going out on my own might look like, I didn't actually know I was going to resign until I did it, more or less in the heat of the moment.

Comfort zones are like that; there I was in a well-paid director's job, working for a charity that did good and purposeful work and was having an impact on many people. I had a strong reputation for my passion and ability to work with, engage and inspire those from tough and challenging backgrounds and helped the charity to its award-winning status. But the volume of work and high expectations, not least placed on me by myself, had begun to take their toll. With constant 80 + hour weeks, driving the length and breadth of the country whilst still trying to be a good dad, partner, son, etc., life was starting to become a bit of a blur. The CEO sat me down one morning in a quiet room at the centre on Skye, and after telling me that even more would be expected of my role in the coming months and years ahead and that she hoped I could raise my game to that of my previous performance, I decided, in that moment, that I had to leave. I could feel the pressure building as she spoke to me. I knew I hadn't been performing at my best for the past few months and I had also gone through a period of anxiety and depression, so I had also been working on autopilot for part of that time. Yet, I was still managing to get the job done to the best of my ability.

I paid attention to my gut during this conversation and could feel it tighten and feel a sense of a huge weight about to be added to the already heavy burden of the role, so, just before the CEO finished her last sentence, I put my hand up, ushering her to pause for a moment. I then said out loud the line I had rehearsed in my head so many times before. "I've decided to leave; you will have my notice by the end of the day."

What was said and what unfolded after the words left my mouth is all a bit of a blur, but what I do remember is a feeling unlike any other, of what felt like the weight of the world being lifted off my shoulders. Sure, there was a sense of panic and of "oh shit! What have I done? What will I do? Omg, I need a wage, etc., etc.," but there was also a real sense of clarity soon after. I knew what needed to be done, I knew how I was going to do it, and I was already curious about what it might look and feel like. I had already spent years training my mind to visualise possibilities and worked on the power of manifesting thoughts into reality and had lots of evidence of this working, so what I really needed to do was what I do best - take action and make things happen.

The following day, I woke up and the first thought I had was, "Man! Today is the first day of working my notice. Shit, I have 7 weeks to make something happen!"

Over the 7 weeks' notice period, my time was going to be split into 2 key priorities: 1. To do a very strong handover and make sure my team had everything they needed to carry things on once I had left. 2. To start my own business, design my own programmes and start bringing in work. It's amazing how liberating handing in your notice can be when you know that what's on the horizon could be your best move yet. That said, fear can also be a great motivator when you know you need to put food on the table and pay the bills!

I had been very curious for many years if I actually had the chops to go it alone and have a successful business that could have the kind of impact that I could picture in my head, where I could make the world just a little better by creating a space and conditions that would allow for real lasting change. It was all becoming very real and the only thing getting between the current situation I was in and my vision was....... well .... me. One of the best lessons I ever learned in my 20s was that sometimes you need to get out of your own way to make things happen. Sometimes, no matter how much we want something, we are indeed the ones that get in our own way by doing one of two things; either not taking the action required or making up excuses. And sometimes it's almost like self-sabotage and we don't move forward because the pain and discomfort we are experiencing are more bearable than the anxiety that can come from taking the leap of faith into the unknown.

I heard this story below from an old friend of mine when I was trying to find the courage to leave the organisation I was in. It pretty much sums up what I've said above but through the story of a whining dog.

Tom just moved into a new neighbourhood recently. He liked his house and his environment, but there was one thing which he didn't get.

His neighbour, Mr Tan, had a dog that kept howling non-stop. Literally. Day in, day out.

"*o o o o o o o o o o o o w w w w ... ... ooooooooooooowww..........*"

Initially, Tom thought the dog was just going through a phase, so he ignored the howls, thinking it would eventually stop.

But it didn't. It continued howling.

"*o o o o o o o o w* ... ... *a u u u u* ... ... *ooooooooww.......*"

1 day passed. Nothing changed. 2 days passed. Still howling. 3 days. 5 days. 1 week. 2 weeks. 1 month. Still howling, with no signs of stopping.

"*ooooooooooww............ooooooooooowww.......ooooooooooww..*"

Finally, Tom couldn't stand it anymore. One fine day, he walked over to Mr Tan's house to see what was going on.

Sure enough, there was the dog, sitting at the front porch, howling pitifully to whoever was walking by.

On the other hand, Mr Tan was relaxing on his bench on the lawn, leisurely reading his newspapers and sipping a cup of coffee.

Wondering what was going on, Tom walked up to Mr Tan.

Tom: "Hi, Mr Tan, is that your dog?"

Mr Tan: "Which dog?" He glanced around. "Oh that. Yep, he's mine."

Tom: "Why does he keep howling?"

Mr Tan: "Oh, that's cause he's sitting on a nail."

Tom: "Sitting on a nail?!?" Tom gave the dog a bewildered look.

"... Okay... so why doesn't he just get away from the nail then??"

"Well, Tom.........", Mr Tan took a slow sip of his coffee before replying.

"...... That's because he doesn't find it painful enough yet."

I think we all have stories similar to this, things that we have stuck with a little longer than we should've because although the pain was present, uncomfortable and even sometimes unbearable, we still sat with it because it was still more comfortable than the unknown.

Curiosity is an incredible tool for personal change, but it's not something that can sit on its own. We can't just sit and be curious about something and hope it will change or come to fruition.

Martin Luther King didn't sit back on his chair and think, "I wonder if I should share that dream I had last night with the world about my four children not being judged by their colour, but by the content of their character." No, he stood up in front of thousands of people, both black and white, and shared his vision for a more equal future and became the most visible activist in the civil rights movement from 1955 until his assassination in 1968.

One of the best tools to use to bring your curiosity to life is to take action, no matter how small. It's the one thing that can undeniably move you from your comfort zone to uncapped possibilities, and from my own experience, there are only two things that will stop you from taking action - fear or laziness. I have been guilty of experiencing both throughout my life, but unlike the whining dog, I've got myself to a place where I no longer let things get too painful before I take action and get moving.

Will Smith has an excellent view on fear and the message he shares is that most of the best things in life lie just on the other side of fear. How many times have you worked yourself up to something that you were hugely fearful of, only to experience the exact opposite once it was over?

One of my biggest fears growing up was speaking in public. Ok, I know this is a huge issue for probably 90% of people, and it usually started in 2nd year where the fear of God was put into us by older students who would ask if you had done your "solo talk" yet. The solo talk was where you had to write about a subject and stand solo in front of the whole class and share your story. I think attendance dropped by over 50% during those days.

Although I had played in bands on stage from a very young age, I was never the frontman, I just stood at the back and played my socks off and didn't really care about being noticed. I just loved the music and playing at our best on every show. But speaking in front of people... no thanks.

It wasn't until I was in my 20s and I started doing group work and began to hone my style of facilitation that I started to find my voice and a way of working with groups. At this point in my life, I have delivered literally hundreds of programmes throughout my 20s, 30s and 40s on everything from leadership to ambition and from Fear to Freedom. Group sizes usually vary and can be anything from 10 – 30 people; usually somewhere in the middle. But every so often, I get asked to do keynote speeches or to be a guest speaker at public events. One such event happened in 2019 when I was asked to speak at an annual conference in Glasgow at the national stadium, Hampden Park. The talk was going to be in front of about 1000 people and was to last about 20 minutes. I am not going to lie; my initial response was actually going to be to say no and that I was too busy. However, I have pushed myself over the years towards trying to say yes to anything that stretches and grows me as a person. But I knew an audience of this size was going to be a challenge and the fear had grabbed me big time. When I am faced with situations like this, there are three things I choose to focus on:

1. Can I physically do it? The answer in this situation was yes.
2. Will it have a positive impact on myself and others? Again, my answer was yes.
3. How do I think I will feel after it? For this particular situation, there was a mix of answers - relieved, proud and maybe even exhilarated. On the night of the talk, I could feel myself physically shaking a little as I walked through the auditorium and saw the rows upon rows of empty seats, knowing the place would soon be jam-packed with people. I went to the bathroom to sit and breathe just for a few moments and did my usual positive self-affirmations.
   - You are Mark Brown, and no one knows your story better than you.
   - You are doing this because you know it will help you grow as a person.
   - When this is over, you will feel strong and proud.

Will Smith was right when he said that most great things in life sit just on the other side of fear. After about 5 minutes of talking on stage, my fear and anxiety subsided, I found my flow and the audience listened intently for the rest of that talk and concluded with a huge round of applause. This evening ultimately led to me being invited to speak to other groups and audiences and it is situations like this where I am so glad that I worked past the fear.

I would like you to take a few moments to think of some of the things that you fear doing, some of the things that hold you back from being the person you know you are capable of becoming or maybe even some of the things that you have always wanted to do but have either been too scared to do or you have just not made a priority.

Either sit back with a cup of coffee and get these things out of your head and onto paper, or, at the very least, put the book down for a few minutes and really think of things that you are putting off due to fear, lack of time or that you just don't prioritise.

Now, once you have identified at least one thing that you are not doing through fear, laziness or whatever, I want you to gift yourself just a few minutes to fantasise in your mind what it would be like to do this thing, to get over the fear or simply to get the things done. It might be speaking in public, having a go at stand up, asking the boss for a raise, leaving that stale relationship, starting up a business, starting a meditation practice. YOU decide, it's YOUR story.

Now take yourself beyond the thing that you want to achieve, imagine what it would be like doing that thing, what will it feel like once you have begun or once you have achieved it. How do you think you will feel after it? Physically say this out loud right now. What will you notice about yourself, what impact has it had and how will you take this even further? I want you to really imagine this in your head; be specific; what will you look like when you're doing it and what will you feel like when you're doing it? Really internalise this for a few moments. The imagination part of this process is the beginning of making it happen. Remember what Einstein said earlier?

"Imagination is everything, it's a preview of life's coming attractions"

In the boxes below, I want you to write specifically what you thought of in these last few minutes.

This process of imagination now takes the ideas out of your head and begins the process of bringing them to life by getting them down on paper. In the following chapters, we will explore getting it off the paper and into reality.

3. Questions to overcome fear

What is it that you're not doing through fear?

What would it be like if you worked through the fear and achieved your goal?

What would it look like?

What would it feel like?

What would be different?

What impact would it have on you and others?

Some days, when I am writing this book, the words and the stories just flow. Others, I sit in front of a blank page and think, 'Why isn't it working today? Will anyone read this? Will lockdown ever end as I write this during the Covid-19 outbreak?'

I don't allow this to last too long, though. Here's how I use the power of my imagination and creativity to get things back on track.

I sit back in my chair for just a few moments. I breathe deeply for 10-12 breaths. And I start a short movie in my head – a little bit like a trailer for a movie I have been dying to see.

In the movie, I am in the office and the door goes; it's a delivery for me. The FED EX guy is standing there with a large cardboard box that looks pretty heavy and he says, "Delivery for Mark Brown?" I take the box and sign for it and take it inside. I take it into the kitchen and use a knife to carefully cut the box open. I peel back the sides of the box, then remove a top layer of paper and then.......... there it is....... a box full of brand spanking new shiny copies of my book with a glossy cover and the title, 'The Best of You' by Mark Brown.

Taking literally one minute to do this in my mind helps the creative side of the process start to flow again as I know the feeling of opening that box full of my published books will far exceed the fear or self-doubt I have right now of whether I should continue or not.

So, please, take the time to sit in silence and start to create your own story of what WILL be possible and not what you think could go wrong. Chances are, your biggest risk will be success....

CHAPTER 3

Victim versus Hero

"Victims take from the world;
heroes give to the world"

~ Robin Sharma

One thing that I believe to be true of all human beings and one thing that I strongly believe connects us all, is that we have a story or several stories in our lives that are worth sharing. Some are good, some bad, some painful, some inspiring, but when we get to a certain age and look back over our lives like chapters of a book, we begin to see our lives like one long story made up of several chapters. I actually don't think you need to be an adult to have a story to share. I have worked with young people in their early teens, many of who were born into tragedy and adversity and they have seen and experienced things that no one should. Yet, when they talk about their back story, you often get a glimpse into why they are showing up the way they do or behaving the way they are.

I think how we share our stories and what we choose to tell about our stories plays a massive part in how we live our lives, who we choose to be and ultimately, what we are known for.

I think for at least two rather significant chapters of my life story, I played a bit of a victim, not something I am proud of but when you don't know any better, it's an easy behaviour to fall into. In this chapter, we will look at how we shift from victim to hero.

In the first couple of chapters, I mentioned my gut health around my diagnosis of ulcerative colitis and how I manage that now, so I am not going to labour this story much further, except to say that there was a long period of my teens when my condition was all that I spoke about and thought about. It also became part of my identity and reputation for a while. When people met me, the first thing they would ask was a very sympathetic, "How's your health doing? Are you ok?" or "How are you coping? Such a horrible illness to have to live with."

Now, to be honest, everyone likes a bit of sympathy from time to time and we all need to know someone cares about us. But I think I had created this identity of always being ill, always in pain and the type of person with daily struggles. It wasn't always directly from me; sometimes it would be my parents telling the extended family that I had had yet another bad flare-up and had been back at hospital or was off school yet again for several weeks. It was not that this wasn't true; it was all true, but fundamentally, it was what I was focusing on that was creating this story. If I fast forward to today, my identity and reputation are very different. The only people that know of my condition are my close family relatives (and those of you reading this book now) and the only time that it comes up in conversation now is if someone from my past asks how my health is doing. Today, this is far more by design than default as I decided during one of my life chapters that this was something that I no longer wanted to be known for. I chose not to be a victim of this condition, but I will come back to that in a minute.

Another time that I believe I played a bit of a victim was in my early 20s. My girlfriend (now my wife) and I had just bought our first flat together. It was the 19th of December 2000 and we were determined to get in just before Christmas, which we did. The flat was an old 60's design based in Cumbernauld just outside Glasgow. It was of a decent size and we couldn't wait to start our lives together there. Two days after we moved in, we received a letter from a local surveyor's company. The letter was addressed to everyone in our block of flats and those in the surrounding area. In short, the letter stated that our flats had suspected structural defects and that they would at some point be rendered unsafe to stay in and ultimately condemned. Now, this is not the type of news that you want to hear, especially two days after you move into your first home and two days before Christmas, but there it was, the flat we had bought was fucked!

Now you would think that there would be something in the legal terms that would have allowed us to get our money back or sue the previous owners or the company we had employed to do the survey, but unfortunately, due to the Scottish legal term of buyer beware, we had no comeback whatsoever. This took years to find out and a lot of money spent on lawyers, advocates and advisers. We ended up staying in this property for 8 years with it literally falling down around us. We had water coming in every room when it rained, parts of the ceiling falling in, the heating wouldn't work, and things were falling off walls as they started to crumble. It was a horrible place to stay, but we had barely enough to pay the mortgage and keep things going, and the flat couldn't be sold due to the defects so we were pretty much stuck there.

The story of the flat became like the story of my health; it consumed me every day. Lawyers' appointments instead of hospital appointments, worrying about money instead of worrying about health, people asking about the flat instead of asking about my stomach. For a while, it felt like it was all I spoke about, and it was never from a positive viewpoint. It was never, "I still have a roof over my head, I still have heating, I still have hot running water and a lock on my door", it was always, "The roof is falling in, there is water coming in every room, we will never get out of this".

I am incredibly grateful for the people who have come into my life at certain points and have asked me the questions that others didn't, or offered me a different perspective of what's going on in my life.

Marie Laidig is one such person who has influenced my thinking massively over the years. I met Marie at an event I was speaking at in my mid-20s. One thing I remember about Marie was that the first thing she asked me about was not my issue with my health or my problems with my flat; no, the first thing she asked me about was my passion for music as it had come up in the talk I was giving, and I used a lot of musical analogy. Marie and I hit it off instantly as we both had, and still have, a huge passion for live music and we have pretty much worked together in many different capacities since.

It didn't take long, when speaking with Marie during our first conversation, for me to start telling the story and off-loading about the situation around the flat and all the woes that went with it, but something that was different about this conversation was that Marie didn't offer sympathy. She didn't offer her opinion and didn't say that line most people chose to finish with; "Oh, that's just terrible, I don't know how you cope".

No, Marie listened to me intently for the duration of my well-rehearsed moan, and once I had finished, simply asked a question.

"So, what are you doing about it?"

This threw me a bit, as no one ever asked questions, they only ever offered their opinion of what they think they would do in the situation. I was used to telling people the story about the situation and about my being a victim, yet again, of some wrongdoing outwith my control and normally being met with,

"Well, they can't do that!"

"I would just sue them."

"That's awful; you'll never recover financially from something like this."

"Just go bankrupt!"

The facts were, they could do that and they did do that, I had tried to sue and lost, and we were not yet ready to throw in the towel and go bankrupt, but no one had ever asked what I was going to do about it in that way.

I could have responded with a list of things that we had already done over the years or talked about the things that we had tried that hadn't been successful, but I sensed this wasn't what Marie was getting at. I do remember giving some half-arsed answer about waiting this out to see what other people affected by this were going to do and that we were going to seek some more legal advice. I think I even said that I was hoping there would be some moral or ethical legal loophole that would make all this better. There wasn't and it didn't.

Throughout that same year, I met Marie a number of times. We would be at the same events or end up working together in some capacity and we became good friends and still are to this day. One day, I was doing my usual moan about the flat and the ongoing situation. At this point, we had been in the flat for about 7 years and suffered financially, mentally and physically, as the cold and damp conditions had taken their toll on the health of both of us. Marie stopped me before I went on anymore and said, "You know, no one is going to come and save you from this, there isn't going to be some happy ending whereby some hotshot lawyer is going to find some loophole and get you all your money back. And there is also not going to be some moral or ethical victory like in the movies if this goes to court. The only way out of this is if you shift your mindset and refocus your energy. You've spent all these years focusing on being hard done to and trying to change what has happened and nothing is working, so you need to decide what you're going to focus on. You can't change the situation, but you have full control over where you choose to focus your energy and you already know what doesn't work, so maybe try focusing on something else?"

That night, I got home in the wee hours of the morning. Although I was working full time, I also played in a band at the weekends to help pay lawyers' fees and all that went with our unique situation. When I got home, I went into the bedroom where my wife Laura was fast asleep. Laura had been very ill off and on, living in the flat with the cold and damp getting into her lungs, resulting in pleurisy. As I looked at her in the bed, I thought I could see smoke around her face, like she was lying in bed having a cigarette to keep her warm (something we had done in the past when it was freezing in the room), but on a closer look, it wasn't smoke coming out, it was her breath in the cold air. The room was so cold yet again that I could see her breathing in her sleep.

That night, I went out to the living room, poured a large glass of bourbon and thought long and hard about what it would look like to refocus my energy and shift my mindset from that of being a victim and hard done to, to one of action and making things happen to get us out of the situation we were in.

When I wrote down the facts and didn't tie any emotion to them, they were clear.

1. We had lost a lot of money trying to fight the case
2. We needed to get out of there and soon
3. My wife and I were extremely resourceful people
4. People have been through and survived much worse than this.

Over the next days and weeks, I decided to focus my energy entirely on one thing - getting out of the flat and to somewhere safe and healthy. We chose to only speak about the present and future and what it would be like to be in a warm and safe house together and stopped talking about what had happened to us and how we had been screwed over by the whole system. Even when people asked how things were going, or if they tried to offer sympathy or support on the situation, we would change our response to one of either "We are making moves to get out of the flat asap", or we would just change the subject.

One of the things I realised during all of this is that it is amazing how much you can influence your situation just by how you view it and what you choose to focus on. Don't get me wrong - it took me a long time to get there - but I saw a difference even after one day of making a deal with myself that I would no longer be a victim of this situation and would no longer be known as "poor Mark, he's been through a lot between his health and what has happened with his flat". I remember, by the end of the first week of not whinging and moaning about the flat, how my energy had changed, and my mindset was becoming one of a more positive outlook and one of what might be possible from here on if I keep focused. I also had to remind myself not to become the whining dog!

Within a few months of practising and honing this new version of myself, and stepping into the action mode of only spending energy on the future possibilities instead of what had happened in the past, we had managed to meet with new financial advisers and had already started to draw on all our resources to make this work and move forward. Don't get me wrong, we were both working like crazy, both in full-time jobs and I was gigging every weekend and teaching guitar in the evenings, and, in addition to Laura's full-time role as a graphic designer, she was also working in a bar at the weekends, all so we could pull ourselves out of the situation. But it is incredible how your energy levels work in your favour when you're not focusing on victimhood and helplessness. In less than one year from making the decision to shift my focus and energy, we moved into a small but perfect ex-council house with heating, hot water and best of all? The walls were not falling down!

I strongly believe that there were only two things that led me to my shift in focus and mindset. Firstly, Marie telling me like it was, as she always does, that no one was going to come and make this right, we had to be our own superheroes to get us out of the situation, and secondly, watching Laura sleep in the cold damp room where I could see her breath and thinking this was only going to get worse and our health had already taken a hit.

It can take a lot of different factors to shift us into a mindset of action; it can be pain, fear, worry, curiosity, willpower, want; it can be different for everyone depending on what the situation is, but for me, the most important thing is finding that mindset and keeping it, no matter what.

When I look over my own back story of coming away from ill health, property issues, relationship issues, anything that felt remotely like victimhood, there is one consistent factor that helped me shift my mindset every time and it's this.... I could always visualize an alternative and better situation to the one I was in, given all that I had practised from a young age, my response to situations that challenged me or felt like they were sent to test me was always to take a big step back and go inwards to visualise what would be possible. Don't get me wrong, sometimes it was a bit like the whinging dog story I mentioned in the previous chapter, and sometimes it really had to hurt first before I would do anything about it, but ultimately, it's what has always moved me from a current reality to a desired one. I think we were born with the gift of imagination for this very reason; this amazing tool that we can access anytime, anywhere, as long as we are willing to look inwards for the answers, that is indeed where most of them lie.

4. Mindset questions

Take a few moments to think about the questions below and allow yourself some inward thinking time to really explore them and what you can imagine changing about your mindset.

1. How would you describe your current day-to-day mindset and what you choose to think about and focus on and does it serve you well?

2. What might you need to change about your mindset in order to achieve the things that are important to you?

3. What are you willing to do to become the person you know you are capable of becoming?

Now, having spent a little time thinking over these important questions, I'd like to invite you to put the book down for a short while, maybe 5 or 10 minutes. If you really want to implement the changes that are possible within this book, then you're going to want to do this next part. Remember what Einstein said, "Imagination is everything, it's a preview of life's coming attractions".

Sit back in your chair or the bed or wherever you are reading this book, eyes closed or not, you are in control. What you think about for the next few minutes is entirely up to you; the only guidance I offer is that you keep it powerful and positive. If any negativity or deficit creeps in, just notice it, acknowledge it and regain control of the story, because it is, indeed, your story.

Ok, so the idea here is to use your imagination to your advantage. There have been many questions and stories in the chapters leading up to this. They have been gently conditioning you to delve into your own mind, your own curiosity and speak to your own inner author to allow you to realise your own potential to become the designer, driver and creator of your own unique future.

Gift yourself some time now to imagine the you of the future, the one that has finished this book and has put into practice everything they have learned and realised about themselves is possible. You decide in this story what you are doing, how you are doing it, who you are with and what it feels like. Remember, it's all positive and it's all possible.

Notice in this story what your mindset is like; notice what is different in your mindset between then and now. What are you focusing on that's different? What have you let go of? Now, just play this out in your mind for a while and come back to the book when you're ready....

CHAPTER 4

Hard as Nails

"Do, or do not, there is no try"

~ Yoda

For as long as I can remember, I have loved movies with superheroes, adventure and inspiring messages. And, as such, I have spent long periods of my life wanting to be like the heroes in these movies. When I was about 6 years old, I remember watching Star Wars for the millionth time and deciding that yes, this was what I was going to do with my life - I was indeed going to be a Jedi!

To be fair, if you asked my wife now, "What do you think Mark would do if he didn't do what he does?" she would probably still say a Jedi, but more on that later.

When I think back to wanting to be a Jedi (we will say it's in the past for now), what fascinated me the most was the use of the Force.

The Force is described as a mysterious energy field, created by life, that binds the galaxy together. Harnessing the power of the Force gives the Jedi, the Sith, and others sensitive to this spiritual energy extraordinary abilities, such as levitating objects, tricking minds, and seeing things before they happen. I know I was not, and am not, alone in wishing I could harness the Force as a superpower to achieve all the above, but I think it was my passion and curiosity about this that led me to study the power of the human mind, spiritual healing, and not so much how to trick people but how to inspire and influence them.

These days, I am probably more like Yoda than Luke or more like Dumbledore than Harry, but my purpose and passion remains the same in that I want to fight for equality, inspire or influence those that I can and generally make the world a better place by helping people realise their own unique potential.

When I founded The Best of You Programme many years ago and after years of working on myself, the strapline to the programme was Dr Seuss's "Why fit in when you were made to stand out?" I still use this quote to this day as I believe it is still relevant.

When I was in high school in the early 90s, I wasn't one for trying to fit in. I wasn't one for really trying to stand out either at that point. I was just trying to get by, but my passion at that time was music. Whilst most of my peers were listening to Oasis, Blur, the Stone Roses and other indie bands of that era, I was listening to blues greats like Buddy Guy, BB King, John Lee Hooker, and my all-time hero, Stevie Ray Vaughan. If I brought these guys up in conversation, I would often get laughed at; "Who the fuck is that?" or "What kind of name is BB?". Still, I loved them. These guys were the blues titans and legends of their time, the storytellers and the ones who created magic on stage where it felt like time would stand still. Apart from Stevie Ray Vaughan, who died in 1990, I got to see pretty much most of my heroes live. As much as I loved their music, their incredibly unique sound and their songs that told stories, what I really loved was the atmosphere that they created in the venue with their audience. This, for me, was where the real magic lay. BB King was a master of stopping his whole band right in the middle of a song because at that very moment, he remembered a story about someone from that song or something that had happened which led to that song being written. He would hold up his hand, the band would all stop and he would launch into this heartfelt narrative which brought the audience to a complete silence, and then, as if by magic, the band would gently pick up exactly where they stopped and bring the song back into full swing, only now, you felt you had a better connection to the song and what he was trying to write about.

I learned so much from these legends over the years around the importance of setting the scene with people, the art of creating conditions for people to feel safe and lock out the outside world if only for an hour or two. This is the kind of atmosphere I try to create on every programme, one where people can switch off from the world for a while and explore what is important to them and find the strength and courage to begin to let go of the behaviours that can hold them back and begin to learn new habits for powerful personal growth.

The one thing I felt, and still feel, that many of these guys have is integrity and authenticity. The older I get, the more I want to spend time with people who offer authenticity and who keep their word. I've grown tired over the years of listening to the often-hyped-up bullshit of people who over-promise and under-deliver.

I have been delivering my Best of You Programmes for over a decade and although the programmes are uniquely delivered to suit the needs of each group I work with, there are some things that are non-negotiable and that I endeavour to keep the same for every single session and programme.

When people sit around the circle for our first session together, these are the three things I say to every group:

1. Be here because you want to be here; don't come each day out of duty, or because you've been told to. Be here of your own choosing and your own curiosity and just experience what shows up for you.

2. If anyone has the courage or bravery to speak out in this group at any point, the rest of us will do one thing and one thing only; we will listen and we will listen without judgement.

3. Only speak the truth; there is no room or need for ego, no need to try and be bigger or better than anyone else, so be authentic and be true to yourself.

Now, don't get me wrong, I am, for the most part, a realist! Working with the types of groups that I work with which often include offenders, addicts, gang members and those that don't normally engage in school, when I share these three guidelines for the programme ahead, they can be met with a vast array of responses, but when I mirror these conditions every day from start to finish and don't waiver from them at all, then this behaviour is ultimately mirrored throughout the group once they realise the power they hold by just being authentic.

When I first meet with groups the week before they come on a programme, there are two aims or outcomes I hope to achieve from this session. Firstly, that I can get an early measure of them as a person regarding their needs and hopes for the programmes and how they might be within the group, and secondly, to ensure that they feel invited and not sent on the programme. It is important that they feel they have a choice in the matter, as this will ultimately dictate how they are throughout the process.

There are many different challenges throughout a Best of You Programme, which I choose based on what stories I am sharing or what subject I am talking about.

Something that I hear people say often is "I'll never be able to do that" or "I will never change, I have always been like this, my dad was like this too so it's in my genes". I often respectfully challenge when someone goes into negative self-talk, but I do it with respect levels high as it can be damaging otherwise. And ultimately, it is that person's current view of themselves and the world and they will not likely change that view unless they are given real evidence that change is indeed possible.

I mentioned earlier that the golden ingredients to all the work and programmes I offer are authenticity and integrity, so when I talk about confidence, motivation and self-belief being possible for everyone, no matter what their back story is, I absolutely need to offer them evidence that this is indeed possible. I do this through the challenges, activities and guest speakers I have on the programme.

One challenge I offer which is a good metaphor for example for showing how the impossible can become possible is the nail-balancing challenge.

In short, I split the groups into smaller groups of about 3 or 4 and give them the same materials; a block of wood with one 4-inch flat-headed nail hammered into it, and 13 other nails of the same size. The challenge is to find a way to balance all 13 nails on top of the one that is already in the wood. They have about 15 minutes and there are 3 rules.

1. All nails must balance on top of the one in the wood
2. None of the nails can be touching the wood or the table
3. You must only use the materials I provide

This is a very interesting challenge in regard to the way people respond. You often get expletives in the first 5 minutes:

"I cannae fucking dae this"
"This is impossible"

"I have no patience, and this is doing my head in"

This inner dialogue is very useful to hear out loud as it gives me an opportunity to evidence how they go from disbelief to belief and from impossible to possible. The challenge is deliberately difficult and is designed to evoke feelings of frustration and test patience, but the real magic lies in how I create the conditions for learning about yourself throughout the challenge and how you feel at the end compared to the beginning, because the challenge is indeed possible, and once you have seen it once, you cannot unsee it, and when you begin to adopt a mindset of how the impossible can become possible, that is where your life can begin to change.

5. The nail challenge

If you have these materials to hand, please feel free to have a go; it's fairly easy to get your hands on one block of wood and 14 flat-headed nails. Hammer one nail in and leave about three inches sticking out of the wood. Then get creative and try and figure out how to balance all of them on the one nail that you hammered in. If you don't have the materials, then just think about how you might try this. If you do try and cannot find the solution (only about 1 in 80 do) then jump on to YouTube and type in 'nail-balancing challenge', and you will see the challenge step by step.

Now, I have been facilitating this challenge for about 20 years, so I am very well-rehearsed at doing the challenge and can therefore complete it in about 30 seconds. This always has the wow factor after participants literally losing their minds by trying for about 15 minutes. I am never doing this to show off or make myself seem smarter than anyone; I always tell the truth that I was given this exercise many years ago and didn't even come close to completing it, but once I was taught the solution, I couldn't unlearn it.

Once I show the group the solution, the narrative completely changes:

"Jesus, that was so easy"

"Man, I can't believe I didn't think of that"

"I got really close, but I gave up at the end"

Again, there is a real richness to this feedback and narrative and it shows the change in belief and mindset in just 15 minutes. They have gone from thinking something is impossible as they feel they have tried everything and some even give up as their patience has hit breaking point. I often use this as a metaphor for life and get into some stories about where else in life this attitude of disbelief can often hold us back and encourage a mindset of one who gives up or even of one who does not try.

I had a teenaged lad on a Best of You programme a few years ago who literally took the materials from this challenge, the wood and the nails, walked over to the window and shouted, "Fuck this pish!" and threw them out the window.

I had a spare set so I gave the rest of the group the remaining time to try and complete the task; this lad sat at the side and watched. After the 15 minutes was up and I took them through the process and noticed him watching intently from the side, once the structure was complete and you could see the solution, I could see his eyes light up.

About 15 minutes after the session was done and the group had left for lunch, I was tidying up my stuff when the lad came back in the room with the nails and wood he had chucked out the window in his hand. He apologised first - "Sorry I threw your stuff away and lost my shit, it's just I don't have any patience for this kind of thing. Any chance you could show me how to build that thing again? It was quite cool, and I want to show my wee brother later; he loves this kind of thing."

I said "Sure, not a problem; thanks for bringing my stuff back, I appreciate it. Also, you don't have no patience. If you had no patience, you wouldn't be showing up here every day, and if you had no patience, you wouldn't sit here for 3 hours listening to me telling stories about whinging dogs.

"I would say you have an awareness that there are some things that frustrate you and you have perhaps told yourself a story that you have no patience, therefore, you should just give up, but someone with no patience would have left this programme on day one and would almost certainly not have taken the time out of their lunch break to go to the back of the school to retrieve my stuff that they threw out of the window."

We sat down, and I slowly talked him through the process of how to complete the challenge. As he placed the last nail onto the pile and found the exact point of balance, he slowly pulled his hands away. I was actually holding my breath praying they would not all collapse as this was a potentially pivotal moment for this lad's belief in himself. As he took his hands away, the nails were perfectly aligned and balancing. He sat back in his seat and very quietly said, "Fuck, that's amazing," and, in that moment, to him, it was indeed amazing. These are the moments that really count on a programme where someone can go from impossible to possible and disbelief to belief in the space of just a few moments and of their own accord.

Going back to the quote by Yoda at the beginning of this chapter, "Do or do not, there is no try".

To this day, I still find this a very powerful mindset to have, as there is something very powerful when we apply an attitude of "getting things done".

Some people will argue that it can be hard to be productive in this day and age where there are so many distractions, probably the biggest distractions being our phones or tablets. I looked at my screen time on my phone a week ago and found out that it was up almost 40% since lockdown, which means I am looking at my phone for an average of 3 hours per day. Now, don't get me wrong; we are in the middle of a pandemic and in a world lockdown, but if I was to take that 3 hours per day and fully allocate it to something of use, like finishing this book for instance, then that would be far more productive than flipping through my Facebook and Instagram. It is moments like this when I put what I teach and share into practice because I know what the end result will feel like. On noticing that my screen time was up by a lot, I started to think about time as a commodity. I was also thinking that although this lockdown is having a hugely negative effect on so many people, families, business, and the economy, it is also giving us the gift of time. There are so many people using this time to do the things that normally they just can't get near - painting the garden fence, repainting the house, learning new skills, running, writing that book!

I made a choice last week that I was going to "do" more not "try" more. I made a small list of what I thought I could achieve in 3 hours instead of looking at my phone. In order to do this, there were just small things that helped; I put my phone in another room, I disconnected my laptop from the Wi-Fi and, I set a timer. By the time the timer had ended, I had cut the grass, washed the car, power-washed the patio and sat down to write more of chapter 4. This is very much a small win but doing stuff like this daily creates a habit, and creating a habit of something you want to do more of or be better at, can only be a good thing.

If you are someone who is easily distracted and sometimes feels like you don't have enough time to do what you want or need to, then try and simplify things for yourself just a little. DO this little challenge below.

6. DO, do not TRY

- Decide how much time you are going to gift yourself
- Make a realistic list of all that you will do in this time
- Get rid of any distractions that may take your focus away from your work and let people know that you will be busy
- Go and DO it and don't stop until you're done
- Once you have completed this list there will likely be a 0% chance that you regret doing any of it and a 100% chance that you will feel some level of achievement and contentment...... off ye go!

CHAPTER 5

To worry or not to worry

"I've had a lot of worries in my life, most of which never happened"

~ Mark Twain

How many times in your life have you uttered the words, "I will be happy when..."?

There can be an endless list of things that we think might make us happy when they happen.

I will be happy when ...

I lose weight

Stop smoking

Get a new job

Get out of this relationship

Get into a relationship

Get a promotion

Come off this medication

When I am no longer depressed

I have also uttered these words at various points throughout my life, however, I did make a conscious decision on how I was going to view certain situations in my life as I knew from an early age that living in the future pretty much means you miss what is right in front of you and happening right now.

I was 17 years old when my then 25-year-old girlfriend said the two words that would change my life forever; "I'm pregnant".

Now, I guess these two words are life-changing at any time in your life, but as a 17-year-old whose only life plan was either to become a Jedi or the next Eric Clapton, this blindsided me a little, to say the least. Within weeks of finding out I was going to be a dad, the relationship had broken down and she said she no longer wanted to be with me. Now, it would be very easy at this point to get into my side of the story and attribute blame and all that goes with it, but I have never found that I, or anyone, gains from this at all so all I will share on the matter is that we separated and I was in contact as much as I could be until the baby was born.

Kristopher arrived on Friday the 3rd of January 1997.

I received a call from his grandmother to say that his mum had given birth and that they were both fine and still in hospital. My dad gave me a lift to the hospital with my mum for us to go and visit and to meet my son for the first time. If you are a parent reading this, you will know that no other feeling quite beats holding your child for the very first time. Even at 17 years old, I felt an overwhelming sense of love and adoration for this tiny little human being fresh out the packet. I also had an overwhelming feeling of responsibility and it felt like in that moment, my priorities changed.

In the months to follow, the agreement was that I was allowed to visit Kristopher at his mum's house under her supervision. This, for me, was not ideal at all as we barely spoke, and I had no experience with babies and was just making it up as best as I could. One thing I noticed after a few weeks of visiting was that I would spend half the week wishing my time away so that I got to hold my son, and then, when I did see him, I was watching the clock the whole time as part of me didn't want it to end and the other part couldn't wait to get out of there as his mum would barely speak to me.

I remember telling this to a musician friend of mine who had been in a similar situation years before and had felt the same. One of the things that he said which really stuck with me was that I would never get this time back and that he regretted not spending more time in the moment with his child and instead, wishing the time away.

I remember thinking about what he said and making the decision that I would make the best of the time I had with him as I knew that the clock was only going in one direction and that I could end up sitting with a 10-year-old who was thinking, "Here I am again with my dad, but he's not really here".

The next few visits, I tried very hard not to focus on the situation or the atmosphere I was in but just my time and presence with my son. I started talking to him more, even though he was only months old. I started to invest my time more in our relationship and manifesting what I wanted it to be and not what it currently was, and I could only do that by being in the moment and making those moments count.

It wasn't until Kristopher was almost 2 years old that I could pick him up in the car and take him out on my own and even that came with its own set of issues as he was so attached to his mum he would often cry or not want to come with me. For me, it was years of patience and baby steps and riding the waves of highs and lows of only being allowed to be a part-time parent that eventually got me to where my relationship with Kristopher is now. At the time of writing this book, he is 23 years old, one of my best friends and someone that I am incredibly proud to call my son.

I have no idea what would have happened if I had continued to wish away my time with him when he was younger, but I am forever grateful that I had the conversation when I did about living in the moment and not letting time get away from me. This, for me, was a life-changing decision.

One of the best ways to live more presently and with less worry is to live your life by acting on what you know and not on what you think you know. As human beings, we are very conditioned to making up stories and filling the gaps when we don't have the full picture.

How many times have you sent a text message only to notice that the recipient read it and didn't respond immediately? And did you resend and say, "Did you get my last msg?" Then, when they still don't get back to you, what do you do? Make up a story of why they are not getting back to you.

Maybe I have pissed them off

Maybe they are not speaking to me

Maybe something is wrong

Shit, I better call them in case they've been in an accident.

Ring ring…

"Are you ok?"

"Yes, why?"

"I texted you twice and you didn't get back."

"Oh, sorry, I got caught up in something, I was going to get back to you later."

Now, this is just one of many millions of stories that we create about situations when we choose to make up stories based on not having all the facts.

When I was in my early 30s, I remember attending an appointment with my consultant about my ulcerative colitis and at the end of the appointment I went to get some blood taken. Once the nurse had taken the sample, she said, "Right, Mark, that's you for another year. Good luck and you will only hear from us if something shows up in your bloods."

"Great," I said and off I went.

To this day, I still get a little apprehensive about going to the hospital when I do, but I always have this massive sense of relief when I walk out the main doors and know that's me for a good long while as long as I look after myself.

On this day, however, I left the hospital and was driving 5 hours all the way to the Isle of Skye where I would be working for the week.

I didn't give the hospital appointment much headspace after I left and actually didn't think much about it at all that week whilst I was away. That was, at least, until I got home on the Friday and there was a message on the answerphone from the hospital.

I got home around 4:30 on the Friday and my wife wasn't in from work yet, so as I began to unpack, I noticed the red light on the answering machine flashing, so I pressed the play button, and these were the exact words:

"Mr Brown, we have your blood results here; could you give me a call when you can?"

Well, I remember exactly how I felt in that moment - my heart stopped as I listened to the 30-second message, then started racing as soon as the message stopped.

My head went right back to Monday morning when the nurse said, "You will only hear from us if something shows up in your bloods".

So, in my head, straight away, the story was that something had shown up in my bloods.

As I mentioned before, when we don't have all the info to hand, often our automatic response is to fill the gaps, make up a story with the little info we have, make some assumptions and then if we tell ourselves the story enough times, it becomes our reality because we believe it to be true.

In this instance, my head was full of all that I knew could be possible with the condition I have and what could have potentially shown up in my blood results. Within 10 minutes of hearing the message, I had come to the conclusion that my white blood count was going to be elevated and that this could be a sign of cancer or that my liver function test was going to be irregular due to the amount of time I had been on the medication, or that my haemoglobin levels were low due to an internal bleed suggesting I was having a flare-up. All these diagnoses were based on a 30-second message from the nurse.

I tried to call the hospital back, but the nurses were away for the day and there was no one there who could give me my results over the phone. This made my panic go into overdrive as I was now not going to learn my fate until Monday morning at the earliest. At that point, I did probably the worst thing you can do when it comes to health and symptoms; that's right, I googled it!

By the time my wife got home, I had diagnosed myself with everything from colorectal cancer to going through the menopause (you may laugh, but, at this point, my mind was in overdrive).

I hadn't seen my wife since Monday morning and when she came in to give me a hug and ask how I was doing, I gave her a sort of half hug and said that there was a message from the hospital and that there was something wrong with my blood results. Already, I had made this worse in my head by believing the story I was creating and, to add fuel to the fire, I was now sharing my fear and my inaccurate story with my wife. She pushed the button and listened to the message.

"Mr Brown, we have your blood results here; could you give me a call when you can?"

"Eh, they didn't say anything was wrong. Why are you panicking?"

"Well, they said on Monday they would only call if there was something, so they wouldn't be calling otherwise, would they?"

"But they didn't say anything was wrong; just don't think about it until Monday and then you'll know when you call them back."

"Aye, right!"

This ever-expanding story was growing serious arms, legs and all sorts of ill-fitting diagnoses of what may or may not be wrong, and I knew for a fact, I wouldn't be switching off anytime soon.

Over the weekend, I played out in my head what I thought the phone call on Monday morning would bring, and what would be said and how I was going to handle the news. I had literally programmed a whole story in my head of what would be said and what was going to happen next. And all this based on a nurse leaving a 30-second message on my phone. By the time Sunday night came, I had actually told myself the story so many times over in my head that I was starting to believe that Monday morning was bringing devastating news. Now, I will pause here just for a moment and share that this is a very dangerous thing to do, create stories like this with potentially damaging outcomes based on very little fact, but at the time, it was a habit of mine, one that had never served me well and one that was about to change.

So, Monday morning came, and I called the hospital at 8:30 on the button. I was put through to the nurse who had left me the message.

"Good morning, Mark, how are you? Thanks for getting back to me."

She sounded a bit chipper for someone who was about to give devastating news, I thought to myself.

"I'm ok. Can you please cut to the chase though and tell me what's wrong with my results? I've been panicking all weekend as I wasn't able to reach you on Friday."

"Sorry, why do you think there's something wrong, Mark?"

"Well, you said on Monday that you would only be in touch if there was something wrong."

"Ah, I see. Sorry about that, I say that to everyone, my apologies. Well, I was actually just calling to let you know that your bloods are looking normal, you appear to be doing very well and are very healthy. Also, I noticed the amount of medication that you are on, and thought we could think about reducing it given how well you are doing."

Long pause from me ....

"So, I'm not dying then?"

Slight giggle from the other side of the phone.

"God, no, why would you think that?"

Anyway, the call came to an end, I hung up with more relief than you can imagine then sat back in my chair and gave myself an internal kicking over the trauma I had put myself through over the weekend based on nothing. I was also disappointed in myself as this was a pattern of behaviour that I would often resort to when I didn't have all the facts to create a clear picture.

I mentioned this story to Marie a few weeks after it happened, and she asked me why I chose to create that story in my head? It wasn't an easy question to answer but I think at that point in my life it was like a default setting. Don't have the full picture? Just make it up, even if it's wrong. Sound familiar?

Marie and I were meeting that day to plan a session we were going to be running for a group later that week and she said she was planning on sharing a tool with the group called the ladder of inference.

I hadn't heard of it before, but Marie said that it actually might be of use for me to learn more about it to combat my default setting of making up unhealthy stories when I don't have all the facts.

We were in a café at this point and Marie drew a ladder with 7 rungs in her notebook and on each rung of the ladder from bottom to top were the words, reality and fact, selected reality, interpreted reality, assumptions, conclusions, beliefs, actions. See pic below.

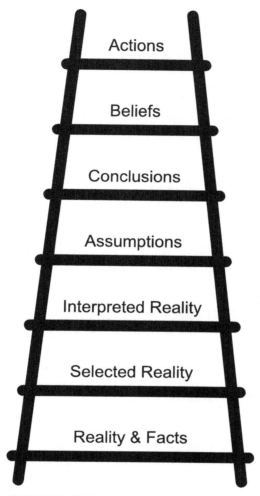

Actions

Beliefs

Conclusions

Assumptions

Interpreted Reality

Selected Reality

Reality & Facts

Concept originally by Chris Argyris

Marie went on to tell me how using this ladder can be a powerful tool for decision-making, and to prevent unnecessary worry.

As I talked Marie through what had happened when I heard the message about my test results, I could see at that moment exactly how my reaction and choices led to me creating my own anxiety based on me choosing to go up this ladder.

Step 1 Reality and Facts

There is a message on the answerphone from the nurse stating they have my results, and can I call them back.

Step 2 Selected reality

I chose to select from memory that I would only be contacted if something were wrong.

Step 3 Interpreted reality

I interpreted this message that something was wrong with my test results.

Step 4 Assumptions

I made an assumption that it would be bad news and that something was indeed wrong.

Step 5 Conclusions

I concluded that I would be given bad news when I called the hospital back on Monday.

Step 6 Beliefs

I told myself this story in detail for the whole weekend and ultimately believed my fate to be true.

Step 7 Actions

I acted in a state of anxiety, spending lots of energy looking for what might be wrong.

Whilst this ladder made perfect sense and mapped out exactly what I had done to myself, I still wasn't sure how to apply it.

Marie asked me at what point did I think I could have stopped myself from getting into panic and worry, and for me, it was on the second rung of the ladder where I was being selective of the information and being selective of the reality. This was where I was starting to distort things and make up a story. It was in filling the gaps with non-facts and then taking it further to making assumptions that what I was telling myself was the truth, and this was something that I had subconsciously learned and created a very strong habit out of over the years.

Marie tore the piece of paper out of her notebook and gave it to me and told me to use it for the next few days. Her instructions were simple; when situations occur and you don't have all the info that you would like and you feel yourself starting to make up a story about it, allow yourself to remain on the bottom rung of the ladder, go with the facts that you have available to you, and if you can find out more facts, then do that, if you can't, don't make up your own facts.

It was amazing how many times a day situations would occur where something would happen, and I would find myself within seconds going to the top of that ladder only to realise that it was me and my constant making up of stories and filling in the gaps that would land myself right at the top that ladder.

I remember, a few days after learning about the ladder, I received a text message from Kristopher, which simply said, "Can't see you today; maybe see you later in the week."

Now, my usual response to that would be to panic, and go straight to the assumption rung of the ladder and make up a story in my head of why my son doesn't want to see me:

"Maybe he has fallen out with me."

"Maybe he doesn't want to spend time with me, the older he gets."

On this day, though, I had in my wallet the ladder that Marie gave me and I brought it out. I already knew I was up on the assumption rung of the ladder, so in order to get back down to the bottom of reality and facts I knew, I needed a little more info, so I called him.

Now, to let you understand, like a lot of young people, Kristopher at that age was not one for big long heartfelt texts. You could send him a big 400-character message and end it with a "so how are you?" and just get an "ok" back and this was very much the case with the message he had sent that day. In short, I was due to pick him up after school to spend some time together, but he had been asked to stay back for a band rehearsal; that was it, nothing less nothing more. Now, by calling him and getting a little more info and using the ladder, I saved myself probably about a day or two of making up stories of why my son no longer wanted to see me.

To this day, I use the ladder on a daily basis. I know for a fact I am less of a worrier for it and also find myself in less drama because of it.

Now, I have simplified and made up my own version of the ladder for working with young people who suffer from anxiety and those who perhaps suffer from overthinking.

My ladder has only 4 rungs; from bottom to top it reads:

1. Stuff happens (We are presented with a situation and some facts.)
2. Story (Based on what we know, we create a story.)
3. Believe (If we tell ourselves the story often enough, we believe it to be true.)
4. Action (We act as if the story were true based on the story we have told ourselves.)

7. Your Ladder

You can decide which version of the ladder suits you the best, but I am going to suggest that you draw your own version of this, or you can go on to Google images and download lots of different versions of this, but print it off and keep it in your wallet or bag and when you find yourself in a position where worry is creeping in, your stress levels are rising, or indeed, you're creating a story which you know is not based on reality or facts, then bring it out and have a look at where you are on the ladder and what you might need to do to bring yourself back down to reality.

It might be that you need to have a conversation, ask a difficult question or be out of your comfort zone and do something that you would not ordinarily do, but you have to decide which is more beneficial to you, asking the difficult questions or sitting with unnecessary worry. Once you have used the ladder for a few days, you will notice that it becomes a habit. Situations will occur and your usual default of making negative assumptions may change to finding out more info before you make a decision on whether to worry or not.

CHAPTER 6

Man in the mirror

"Stop acting as if life is a rehearsal, live this day as if it were your last. The past is over and gone and the future is not guaranteed"

~ Wayne Dyer

I find it a real privilege and pleasure to do the work that I do.

I have been delivering personal development programmes in one way or another for almost 20 years, with the last 10 years taking me all over the UK and some parts of Europe.

Although the Best of You Programme was originally designed for young people from tough and challenging backgrounds, it wasn't long before other services supporting adults heard about the programme and asked to meet to explore if the programme would be relevant for their service-users. Over the past decade, the programme has been delivered to adults who have been through the criminal justice system, women who have survived domestic violence, adults with mental health issues and those who have been long-term unemployed.

Working with "criminals" can feel like a daunting task at first. When I first started offering programmes to this service, staff would often send me a huge background report on the people who would be attending the programme. The report included past offences, offending behaviour, history of violence, a list of charges and this could be anything from murder, rape, sex offences, fraud, theft, in fact, pretty much an endless list of offences.

It can be difficult to enter a room with a non-judgemental attitude when this is what you're going to be faced with, so, after a few of these programmes, I asked staff to stop sending the reports as they were not helpful and made it tricky not go straight to the top of that ladder and make up horrific stories of what might happen on a programme if things went wrong.

With this type of group, I had to prepare myself emotionally and mentally before starting the sessions. I would always meet them the week before the programme began to introduce myself and agree on some boundaries and guidelines that we would all stick to, to ensure a safe atmosphere and a powerful experience.

The only rules I have for this type of programme are:

- Do not discuss your past offences during the sessions in any way. With respect, I have no interest in your past, only your present, and where we go from here.
- Do not arrive under the influence of alcohol or any illegal substance. If you are high or drunk, the programme will have no impact and will just be a blurry memory.
- Do not speak on behalf of other people, only speak on behalf of yourself.

I would say that more than 95% of people who have been through the criminal justice programme that I run are remorseful for what they have done and just want to move on with their lives. I have met the odd one that enjoys the criminal lifestyle and enjoys the excitement of living on the edge, or at least that's what they say.

Although I say at the beginning that I am not interested in their past, I am really referring to their criminal past; their past life story is always of interest and can always be of great use when trying to understand a set of behaviours and beliefs.

I often find that if someone is truly up for changing, then they will put in the work to do just that. A bit like giving up smoking, with some people it can several attempts and with others they do it first time, but when the stakes are high and the conditions are right, even the most damaged or hard-wired beliefs and behaviours can be changed.

A bit like you reading this book, you may have read the title and thought 'hmmmm, "The Best of You", I want some of that,' or 'I want that version of me back,' or 'I could do better,' or 'I am not yet living my true potential,' or maybe you thought the book was about Dave Grohl from the Foo Fighters! Either way, it was probably your curiosity that made you pick the book up. You may have already noticed that by taking the time to think about and answer some of the questions in this book, you are noticing some change already.

The first step to making any lasting change is to firstly have a self-awareness of what it is we want to change and why we want to change it.

Around five years ago, I was running a programme in the beautiful Kingdom of Fife in Scotland. The programme was attended by 8 men who were all going through the criminal justice system. This was a challenging programme on many levels as the group had a high percentage of men with mental health problems and a history of serious drug abuse.

One lad on the programme, who I will call John, was in his early 30s and was attending the programme with a view to gaining employment thereafter.

On speaking with John throughout the week, he shared that he had been through the care system (as many offenders have) since he was 3 years old and that he had served his first sentence in Polmont Young Offenders at age 16, and then moving on to Saughton Prison in Edinburgh in his early 20s. When John spoke about his childhood, it was as if a dark shadow came over him and the curtains of his mind started to close like he was shutting down. John became a young father at 17 and when I shared that I was also a young dad at the same age, we started to connect a bit. The only time John ever lit up was when he was talking about his daughter, who he had not seen for about 10 years, or when he was talking about music. My own passion for music and use of musical metaphor throughout the programme allowed us to connect enough to have powerful conversations during the time on the programme. The two biggest issues holding him back were his history and his view of himself. If you asked John about how he viewed himself, he would tell you he was a waster, a loser, a junkie and a criminal. It's at points like this on a programme where I have to hold that space when someone says things like that very carefully. These comments cannot sit in the air for too long without being spoken about or respectfully challenged or they can further cement one's belief about themselves. And with the type of people, both young and old, who attend my programmes, these views on self are often aired in one way or another throughout the programme. When John shared this during the programme, the rest of the group sat back in silence and let him have his space. Some were quietly nodding, with an "I feel the same, mate" kind of agreement and some sat waiting for me to say something that was going to make him feel better about himself. Whilst there is nothing wrong with making someone feel better about themselves in these moments by telling them what they need to hear, it can often be a short-term fix to a long-term issue. Instead, in these situations, I have a process to take people through that allows them to explore how they might hope others might see them and how this can influence how they see themselves.

On this day, I decided to ask the whole group to sit back for a few moments and think of this situation, and yes, I am going to ask you to do the same at this point in the book.

8. How others see us and how we see ourselves.

You don't have to have seen the movie to do this exercise, but in Harry Potter and the Philosopher's Stone, there is a scene where Harry is given a cloak of invisibility. This cloak allows Harry to go about unnoticed, but he can see and hear everything that is going on around him.

Now, I want you to take a few moments and think about a few people throughout your life who have mattered to you and you believe you mattered to them. It doesn't matter if it is a family member, a partner, a teacher, friend or co-worker, just picture them in your mind for a moment. Also, think about why they mattered to you or why they were important to you. Was it something they did, or said or were they a good listener, or did they look after you or maybe give you a kick in the arse when you needed it? Just allow yourself to think about them for a few moments. For the next few minutes, I am going to ask that you focus only on the positive and not on the negative, so, if anything negative does pop up, just allow it to pass and then refocus on the positive.

Now, you may have your eyes closed as you do this exercise; sometimes it is easier to picture things in your mind's eye with your eyes closed, but it is up to you, you are in control of your story.

Imagine that you have your own cloak of invisibility and you put it on and you enter a room holding all the people you were thinking about who matter to you. It doesn't matter if there were only two or if there were ten (if there was only one, imagine them speaking to someone you don't know). Now, bear in mind they cannot see you at all but you can hear everything without them knowing you are there.

As you get closer, you notice that they are talking about you and you may even be surprised that what they are saying is very positive. Allow yourself to create a story right now about what you hope you would hear these important people in your life saying about you. It doesn't matter if these people are from your past or your present, what matters is that they are sharing stories about you and how they have admiration for how far you have come and what you have survived and what you are striving to achieve, (these are just some ideas) but really allow yourself to fantasise about what amazing things these people would be saying about you - remember, it's your story and you are in control. Now, after listening in to this conversation about how proud these people are of you, you decide to leave and let them finish their conversation as you head out of the room to digest a little of what you have just heard. As you stand there in the hall, you notice another room and you can hear some more familiar voices and you are compelled to keep your cloak on and go and explore a bit further. As you enter this room, you notice someone who looks very like you and, as you get closer, you realise it is you! It's the you of today and he's talking to a much younger version of you! In fact, as you look around the room, you notice that the room is full of different versions of you all throughout your life, but you recognise every single one.

Now, this may feel a little strange and possibly even a little uncomfortable, but take some time now to sit back and, in your imagination, tune in to what you hear from all these versions of yourself. Remember, there are no negatives allowed at this point, only the good stuff!

Just as a guide, imagine what the younger version of you might be asking or saying to an older version of you and imagine how the older version might respond. Think about how they might support each other and how a younger version of you might appreciate some words of wisdom from an older you and how the older more mature you might offer some reassurance that things will and do get better, there are always ups and downs, good and bad, but so far you have survived every single thing that has come your way. Allow yourself to really tune in to all these versions of yourself and hear the stories and comments about all that you have achieved, have overcome, have dealt with and have survived and know that all these versions of you are on your side and will continue to help you become the absolute best version of you.

Now, taking a step out of the room having heard all that has been shared about you, gift yourself some time to take this in and allow the time to immerse yourself in how these people and all the versions of you really see you. This is not an easy task, especially if you have held yourself in low regard for many years, but by taking the time to do this, it will begin to rewire some of these old stories and views you hold.

When I took John and his group through this process, I knew there was a lot of discomfort coming up for a lot of them, in particular, John found it hard to think of anyone that he thought he mattered to and vice versa. When he eventually settled on his daughter and an old social worker that he seemed to have a good relationship with, he shared that he pictured them having a conversation about him and they were saying how well he had done and that against all odds he had left his old life behind and carved out a very positive future. He even took his story a step further and fantasised that his daughter then said to the social worker that she couldn't stay long because she was going to meet her dad! The mind is a powerful tool for change when we gently take back control one thought at a time.

About two years ago, I was back working in the Kingdom of Fife, this time with a school group. I had two programmes running that week so only had time for a quick coffee in between sessions ending and starting. I popped into a coffee shop, ordered my Americano and was asked to take a seat and my coffee would be brought to my table.

A few minutes later my coffee arrived and the lad serving it said,

"Marko!"

Immediately, I recognised that it was John from the programme.

He looked great, he had put on a bit of weight, he'd had his hair styled, his skin looked better and all-round he just looked like a happier soul.

He sat at my table for all of a few minutes and told me how he had finished his community service, hadn't picked up any offences since I had last seen him and, even more importantly, said he couldn't stay long as he was about to finish his shift and was going to meet his daughter. They had reconnected a few years ago and done a lot of work to get to know each other again and were taking things slowly but all in all, this was a changed soul who was clearly on a journey that was allowing him to see himself differently.

When I try and describe the "why" around doing the job that I do, it is stories like this that are like the payday; this is the reason I get out of bed in the morning and work hard to create conditions for every single group and person on a programme. Playing a tiny part in someone's story to help them become what they are capable of is the richest form of wealth there is for me.

CHAPTER 7

What is *your* South Pole?

"Champions never complain, they are too busy getting better"

~ **John Wooden**

In 2004, I was running a leadership programme on the Isle of Skye.

The group I was working with were all from Glasgow. Most were recovering addicts, some of them were using the heroin replacement drug methadone and others were living in homeless accommodation in the city centre. I had worked with this group for a few weeks running up to the residential element of the programme and had prepared them as best as I could for what I knew was going to be a challenging week for them.

As part of the programme, we would often take the group to some of the most scenic and beautiful parts of the island, the Old Man of Storr, Fairy Glen, the Quiraing and Staffin Bay, to name a few. On this particular day, we decided to take the group to the Old Man of Storr so that they could experience a different atmosphere from our leadership centre and begin to have deeper conversations about their hopes for their time on Skye. Although not quite a Munro, the Old Man of Storr has an elevation of 719 metres, and if you've never climbed a hill of any great height before, then this is a challenging climb.

We all got out of the minibus and grabbed our bags. Pretty much the whole group lit up a smoke before they began their walk and already there were a few moans and whinges about the walk ahead as they could see the summit at what seemed to look like miles uphill.

We walked for about 30 minutes and stopped for another smoke and drink of water then would start again and walk on for about 30 minutes at a time. By the time we got about 150 metres from the summit, 3 of the group had decided to go back to the minibus and the remaining group were in full whinge mode about sore feet, sore back, wet jackets and cigarettes that wouldn't light due to being soaked.

As we stopped at the last rest place before hitting the summit, one of the lads launched into a rant about us making them walk in these conditions and what was the fucking point of going up to see a big fucking rock in the pishing rain! His anger was spilling over to the group and he was slowly building his little empire in the moment, making it clear he wanted to lead his friends down the hill before reaching the top. As is always the case in these situations, there are opportunities to learn, grow, challenge, or indeed, give up. I gave the group the choice of heading back to the warm minibus and we could head back to the centre for some hot soup and a cup of tea. I handed the decision over to them with only one short statement that they were 15 minutes from the top and that this may be the only time in their life that they would get to see and experience what is considered one of the most beautiful sights in Scotland. The group murmured to each other for all of 30 seconds and then their spokesperson stood up and said "Nope, let's get down this hill; it is getting wetter, and we can see a nice view from here …. And we want some soup"!

Happy with their decision, they turned around and were just about to start the descent back to the minibus, when about 50 feet in front of them, heading up the hill and running toward them… yes, running, was an elderly gentleman with a bald head and a long white beard. "Fuck me, Santa is on his way, troops!" The group erupted into laughter as the old guy drew closer, and when he was within talking distance, he paused for just a few seconds and asked the group how Storr was looking from the top today. "Eh, we've not been yet," said one of the lads.

"Oh, well, you're minutes away, guys, and I promise you won't be disappointed; it's spectacular. See you later!" and off he went, and the lads watched him run up the last few hundred feet towards the summit.

The lads stood in silence for about 30 seconds before one of them said, "How the hell is someone of that age running up this hill, no even out of breath?"

Another said, "How can anyone of any age run up this hill?"

Just as they finished their cigarettes, they noticed the old guy reach the top, touch the large rock that represented Storr and then start running back down towards them.

"How old do you think he is?" one of them asked.

"Dunno, at least 70, I would say" another offered.

"Am gonna ask him when he passes."

"Fuck it, will we just do this last wee stretch and see what he's talking about?" and off we went for the last few hundred feet of ascent.

It was only about 2 minutes of walking uphill before we met the old guy again. He was running, but taking his time as the ground was a bit uneven, and as he got closer to the group, he shouted, "Good choice, lads!"

"Here, mate, how old are you?" one of the lads shouted.

"Ha! Today is the 49th anniversary of my 21st birthday" he shouted, and off he went jogging carefully back down the hill.

There was a silence for about 30 seconds where you could almost hear the cogs turning in the lad's heads as they tried to figure out the maths,

"Fuck me! That old guy is 70 years old," one of them shouted.

At that, the group grabbed their bags and started walking a little quicker and in dead silence to the top of the hill. The sore feet and drenched jackets didn't seem to carry as much weight as before and within 10 minutes, we were all standing at the very top of the Old Man of Storr.

We were there for about 30 minutes and there were a few coffees and cigarettes shared and lots of talk about "that old man" and how could someone be that fit at that age.

Having been to the top of that hill many times, I used my time to let the group relish in their achievement and find a quiet spot to meditate just for a few moments.

Storr is a magical place, and if you have not yet been, I suggest you add it to your bucket list.

As the group walked back down the hill and headed towards the minibus, there was a noticeable calm and sense of peace within the group. Getting to the top, when they thought they couldn't, meeting the old guy who, at age 70, was fit enough to run the hill and experiencing a literally breath-taking view for the first time was something that these guys had never really experienced in their lives.

Later that night, the rain stopped just enough for us to head down to Staffin Bay and have a fire on the beach. As part of the programme, we would always encourage people to spend about 30 minutes journaling at the end of each evening by way of making sense of their day and, if they chose to, to share part of that with the group. As we went round those who wanted to share a little of what they had written, you could hear some themes emerging around regret and giving up and lacking in perseverance for certain things in life, but there was a shift in their story today, as it seemed meeting the old guy near the top helped them shift their mindset and make it to the top. One of the lads actually asked if it was a setup and did we know the old guy and ask him to show up for groups that were struggling to get to the top? This raised a little giggle around the fire, but all I shared was that sometimes the right people show up just at the right time.

The following morning, the centre leader shared with me and the group that we were to have a very special guest later that day and that we should amend the programme itinerary in order for us all to be there to meet with this person in the hall at 3 pm. I had no idea who was coming but was told it was someone who had been on the programme the year before and had just done something extraordinary.

That afternoon, we were set up in the hall and waiting for our special guest. The centre leader came in with the guest and they sat in front of the projector screen and we were introduced to Craig Mathieson, Polar Explorer.

Craig had just returned from leading the first successful Scottish Expedition to the South Pole!

He spoke to us for over an hour about the preparation and training it took and the mindset he had to take on the journey that only a handful of human beings have survived.

He talked about the importance of not doubting yourself and having an attitude of "If you think you can, then you will, but if you think you can't, then you will probably be right about that too."

The room was completely silent for the duration of the talk and the lads from our programme sat in complete awe of what they were hearing.

Inspiration was not something this group were used to but having achieved their goal of reaching Storr the previous day, meeting the old runner on the hill and meeting Scotland's greatest living explorer, things were beginning to change.

After Craig had finished his talk, we invited him to join us for a fire and a private Q and A with our group.

One of the lads asked Craig about his upbringing and said that he assumed he had a good background and motivational parents and had a good education which got him into a good job.

Craig shared that in actual fact, he felt he had a very privileged upbringing and that he was born into a travelling family. One of the lads asked, "So you are a gypsy, then?"

"Yeah, something like that," Craig answered.

He also shared that school just wasn't for him and that having severe dyslexia held him back a fair bit. One thing that really struck a chord with the group was when Craig said that coming from a travelling background, when it came to reputation, mud really would stick. "Once a thieving gypo, always a thieving gypo," was a typical comment that Craig endured throughout his teens. But it was, in fact, a teacher that gave Craig the book 'The Worst Journey in the World' by Apsley Cherry-Garrard, the memoir of Captain Scott's ill-fated expedition to the South Pole, and it was on reading this story aged 12 years old that Craig decided that one day, he would reach the pole himself. The Q and A with Craig went on well into the night and Craig eventually left and was setting up camp with his son just a short distance from our centre.

We were preparing to have just a short review of our day around the fire like we did each night. Around 10 pm, we would gather in a circle and myself or one of the other facilitators would begin the review using the Native American Talking Stick. The Talking Stick is a tool used in many Native American Traditions when a council is called. It allows all council members to present their Sacred Point of View. The Talking Stick is passed from person to person as they speak and only the person holding the stick is allowed to talk during that time period. We would use the talking stick in a similar way, whereby one of the facilitators would pose a question to the group, and we would pass the stick around the circle and each person would have the opportunity to have their voice heard, and only one voice at a time was permitted.

Although everyone was exhausted on this particular night, every single person had something to share. Some said they were still revelling in their achievement of reaching the top of Storr, some said they were still in disbelief about the old guy's age who was running up the hill and many were still sitting in awe of what they had heard from Craig Mathieson.

The final person to share their voice using the stick that night shared a quote from author JK Rowling which was:

"It matters not what someone is born, but what they grow to be."

This became a powerful theme of conversation for the rest of the programme and something that became a powerful message to each of the group. Most of this group had indeed been born into poverty, addiction and in geographical areas of multiple deprivation. But the narrative of this story was beginning to change based on what and who they were experiencing during this programme. The programme came to a powerful and emotional close on the Friday and we waved them off as they began their 6-hour bus journey back to Glasgow.

I checked in with this group many times over the following year and whilst some struggled with the idea that they could be equally as powerful people in Glasgow as they were on Skye, there were others who decided to devote their next chapter to being their best yet. Two of the group ended up volunteering at the leadership centre for a year, one went on further expeditions with the Ocean Youth Trust and some we never heard of again. This was always the challenge of being a small charity with a small number of staff; no matter how powerful a programme was, it was always afterwards that the real work for people began and where the support was really needed.

After I left this charity and started up my own company, I reconnected with Craig and was keen to meet up and see how his life had unfolded after his South Pole expedition. Craig and I met for a coffee and he shared that since we had last met, he had been on many expeditions and that one expedition had had a profound impact on him and what he was now going to do with his life and career.

Craig had trained a young lad called Christopher from Grangemouth to become a young explorer. Chris had been struggling at school and had been at the receiving end of severe bullying and was on a downward spiral to a less than positive future. A chance meeting outside the head mistress's office led to the pair having a discussion about Chris's future and what might be possible for him.

Craig met Chris's parents and they agreed to let him train their son for a year to take part in an expedition to the geographic North Pole. No Scottish teenager had ever taken on such a challenge, and if successful, Chris would be the youngest person in history to complete this journey.

After months of training and Craig teaching Chris how to navigate, ski, and survive in one of the world's harshest environments, they were ready to take on the expedition. It took two weeks of skiing for 8 hours per day through the toughest of conditions, including porridge ice, which is like frozen quicksand, ice breaking up underneath them due to global warming, and temperatures of below -30.

There were points where Chris said he struggled with tiredness and fatigue, but there were rules on expeditions with Craig, two of which were no moaning and no giving up. He also knew how much training and time he had put into this, and that if he made it, it could potentially change his life. After two weeks, they reached their destination, all in one piece, safe and ahead of schedule.

When Chris arrived back at his school a week later, the whole school came out to the playground to clap him in, even the lads who had been bullying him. Chris's life was indeed changed due to the decision he made to take on the challenge. Weeks and months went by and Chris used the same mentality for his school work as he did for his training for the pole and ended up doing much better than anyone thought possible in his exams. This ultimately led him to University and gaining a 1st class degree in Geology. Chris now lives in New Zealand and lectures in Leadership. Not bad for a 16-year-old who was heading for troubled times.

After Craig and Chris successfully reached the North Pole and returned to Scotland, Craig handed in his notice at the accountancy firm that he had just been made partner in, took 100% pay cut and started up the Polar Academy. This has turned into one of the most unique youth charities in the world whereby Craig travels all over Scotland and finds the other Chris's who are heading down a tough road to a challenging future and then selects a group of 10 young people and trains them for a full year to become the fittest and best versions of themselves before taking them on a life-changing expedition to unexplored areas of Greenland. This charity is now in its 10th year and has also been the focus of a BBC documentary – The Arctic Academy.

Craig is a good friend of mine and has also been a guest speaker on about 90% of my programmes since I started up 10 years ago.

Having guest speakers such as Craig on the programme, and giving people evidence of what human potential looks and feels like, is an incredible way to spark people's curiosity about their own potential; whilst some people leave these talks wanting to become the next polar explorer, others leave with a deeper question about what it is they really want to be known for.

One thing that I have learned since starting my own company, and especially when I think about the impact that I am trying to have on people and on my own personal growth, is the importance of surrounding myself with the right people. We have all heard of and have probably experienced "energy vampires" at points in our lives and some people can be very attracted to other people's drama, but one thing I know is true the older I get, is that those who enjoy the drama, the moaning, the bringing other people down, get very little done and often never find their own greatness and potential, whereas those that don't think too much about what others think of them and those that avoid drama and don't whinge when life throws them a few curveballs tend to have much more fulfilling and purposeful existences.

When I was making some changes to my own behaviour around my reactions and responses to certain areas in my life, I remember a mentor of mine challenging me not to moan or whinge about anything for one week and to just be aware if anything was different.

I took on this challenge armed with only a journal to note what came up throughout the week.

One of the first things to happen on day one of this challenge was that a proposal I had been working on for a large contract, which felt like a sure thing, was rejected with no feedback offered. My usual response to something like this would probably have been to moan and maybe go off on one about the number of hours I had put in and then maybe get into blame a little bit, accusing them of not valuing the programme or indeed the people it was going to be for. Instead, I noted down what had happened and decided not to respond in any way. I didn't email them asking for feedback, I didn't even mention it to my wife. I just let it be and tried not to think about it too much.

The same week, someone drove into the back of my car at a roundabout and I had to send the car to get repaired, pick up a rental, deal with insurance and all that goes with things like this happening. Again, I made a conscious effort not to moan and overreact to the situation.

During that week, there were other small things happening that I would normally have moaned a bit about, from schools not responding to emails, to the sale of my guitar not going through, to someone covering our front door in jam…. yes, jam!

Because I knew I was taking this challenge seriously and was working hard not to overreact and moan, I did my very best to accept these things as just situations that I had no influence over. By the time it came to the end of the week, I remember going out to the garage to grab a bottle of red wine from the fridge (yes, I like my red wine chilled); as I turned round, the bottle flew out of my hand and smashed on the ground. Now, those who know me well, know how much I enjoy a glass of red wine at the weekend, and normally, this would warrant a momentous moan and potential overreaction about the situation, especially given all the other stuff that had gone on that week, but as it happened, before the wine had even started to seep into the concrete (no I didn't grab a straw), I found myself reaching for the kitchen roll and the brush without uttering a word or moan.

This surprised me a little, as normally, I would have had a 30-second rant about losing a nice bottle of red and the big pink stain on the garage floor, but I just cleaned it up and got on with it. I remember speaking about it with my mentor the following week and she shared that this was as a result of spending just one week programming a new response to when things don't always work out or when things catch us off guard. Every time we choose to react differently or not to react at all, we create a stronger neural pathway to this behaviour and it ultimately shows up in the form of a habit. And having the habit of not moaning and not overreacting can very much lead to a much better and more relaxed version of ourselves.

9. How to stop overreacting in the moment.

This challenge or piece of homework is something to try over the next week and I urge you to try this every time something comes up that you know you might always react to or have a moan about.

When something happens, and you feel yourself about to react, it doesn't matter how big or small the situation is, but as you feel yourself starting to react, ask yourself these two questions below, and then make a conscious decision on whether you still want to react the same way or not.

- How much will moaning or overreacting help this situation?
- Will this matter in a few days or weeks from now? (if the answer happens to be yes, refer to question 1 again)

If you can, note down all the times that things happen and what your reaction and responses were at the time. The more you practice the art of non-reaction and not moaning about stuff, the more you will notice how much calmer you are, how focused you can be, just how much you can achieve and how far you can go when you don't moan as much.

CHAPTER 8

Have we met?

"Dear past, thank you for all the lessons, dear future, I'm ready now"

I've thought long and hard about whether to write what I am going to share in this chapter or not, as it is going to be very much a "down the rabbit hole" chapter, but I don't think I can give a full picture of my story and give some insight into the real power that the human soul has without sharing this, so, hold on to your hats.

In my early 30s, I was spending a lot of time working with gangs and groups of young people from inner cities. As part of the programme, I would share effective ways of managing conflict and having powerful and meaningful conversations. I would always do as much research as I could on a subject or workshop I was planning and make sure the content was of great value and would ultimately be extremely useful for those I was teaching at the time.

One night, I was doing some research into gang culture in Scotland and I ended up reading about the knife amnesty in Easterhouse in the late 60s.

One of the UK's biggest pop stars at the time was the late Frankie Vaughan. Frankie Vaughan had sung in Glasgow venues many times, but one night, whilst singing at the Barrowlands, he lost his voice, and instead of shouting abuse and complaining, the audience decided to sing the rest of the song for him and cheer him on. This was one of many reasons that Frankie fell in love with Glasgow. Frankie did, however, struggle with how Glasgow was portrayed to the rest of the UK as it was being dubbed as a slum full of angry and violent people with high levels of crime everywhere.

In 1968, Frankie decided to visit Easterhouse, a housing estate in the east end of Glasgow, notorious for its gang culture. Frankie met with local gang members to try and understand what led them to live the often-violent existence of gang life. He was met with lots of reasons, from family history, loyalty, football preferences and religion, but the underpinning message he was hearing was that there was nothing to do around the estate and boredom played a big part in the behaviour.

Frankie made a deal with the gang leaders and said that if they all handed their knives and weapons in to the police and stopped the gang violence, then he would commit to building them, and fully funding, a community centre in Easterhouse. The project was a success; thousands of weapons were handed in, and true to his word, Frankie built them a youth club community centre, and violence did cease in the area, at least for a while anyway.

As is often the case when time passes and funding comes to an end, the community centre eventually closed, and the violence and gangs returned. Frankie Vaughan died in 1999 and a few years later, his son, David Sye, heard that they were going to try and revamp the community project and offered his support as he had been to Glasgow with his father many times before and knew of his father's passion for the community. David was, and still is, a world-renowned yoga teacher and uses yoga as a tool to manage conflict all over the world. He has delivered his world-class Yogabeats retreats all over the world, including war-torn countries like Bosnia and the west bank. His mission is to make the world a more peaceful place through the use of yoga and his work is also endorsed by his holiness, the Dalai Lama. The more

I read about David Sye, the more I wanted to find out about him. I was curious if he might be someone that could help me have a deeper and more spiritual impact with some of the gangs I was working with.

The very next day, which happened to be Christmas Eve, a friend of mine sent me an email with an attachment which simply read, "The bad boy of Yoga" and my friend's email subject said, "Thought you might like this".

The attachment was an article which had been written about David Sye and his mission to change the world through yoga.

Now, I never have believed in coincidence, and favour more the idea that things often happened just at the right time and for the right reason. Also, I hadn't heard from my friend in a long time, let alone speak to him about the research I had come upon the day before, so it was indeed very strange to receive an email about David Sye which had no possible connection to the day before.

Anyway, I read the article with great interest, but the piece that got me the most excited was where the interviewer asked David what led him to yoga and why he had started it in the first place. It turned out that in his 20s, he was diagnosed with ulcerative colitis and had many tumours on his colon. He was destined for surgery as his case was severe, as mine had been in my teens. Before committing to surgery, David had heard about some Tibetan healers and wanted to meet with them before he had part of his stomach removed. He met with the Tibetan healers and agreed to spend some time with them where he went through a series of transformational and healing processes which included Tibetan rebirthing and revealing breathing sessions and yoga movements and poses which allowed his inner energy to become unblocked and move more freely. After a period of time spent with the healers, David returned to the hospital where they found no tumours and very little evidence of the previous diagnosis. This was the point where David's life changed, and he devoted his life to yoga.

As I mentioned, I do not believe in coincidence, and I felt like the universe was perhaps ushering me in a direction to make contact with this yoga dude, so, as I was finishing work for the Christmas break, I thought I would call the number on his website, leave a message and hopefully set up a conversation with him in the new year. To my surprise, David himself answered the phone. I was a bit surprised as I expected to either get an answering machine or perhaps a receptionist, but it was the man himself on the other end of the line. Before getting into any preamble, David immediately recognised my accent as Scottish and asked if I was from Glasgow. Within seconds of being on the phone to him, he launched into a full-blown passionate account of some of his trips as a child with his dad to Glasgow and how he loved the people there. I don't know if you have ever met someone and felt like you know them from a previous life or something like that, but that was very much how I felt after just a few minutes on the phone to him. David and I spoke for over an hour on this first phone call and I was struck by his openness about his life and his work with someone who had just rung out of the blue and on Christmas Eve! At the end of the phone call, I asked David about how he managed his condition now. "What condition?" he asked.

"Your ulcerative colitis."

"Aww, man, that's long gone."

"Cured, you mean?"

"Yeah, something like that. Look, you sound like a good guy doing good work up there, so if there's anything I can help with, just gimme a shout; I would love to come back to Glasgow."

Wow, I couldn't believe this guy who I'd only known for an hour on the phone was offering his support for the work I do and that I would actually get to meet him.

"That would be amazing, man, yeah, let's make something happen and I'll get some funds together to get you up here" "Oh, one last thing, could you tell me a bit more about this Tibetan rebirthing session that you went through and how I can find out more about? You see, I have the same condition and I work hard to keep it at bay and under control so I would love to know more about the process."

"Tell you what, man, can you afford to get down to London at any point? I have a small flat in London and if you want to go through the process, I will take you through it. I trained to do this after I went through my own healing sessions, but I will tell you this, if you go through it, you have to be prepared for what will come up and you have to be prepared to do something with what you learn about yourself."

This was beginning to feel a little bit like a conversation with Yoda and that he was about to teach me the ways of the Force, so, of course, I was in!

David describes revealing breathing (Tibetan rebirthing) below:

What is it?

A combination of Tibetan Re-birthing, healing and shamanism, it is a technique to access the deeper subconscious information layered within and beneath the surface personality. When the body remains still, and a continuous cyclic breathing is applied, the resultant energy within the body stimulates the organism into automatic repair and what is released is the thought forms and ideas held within the subconscious mind. Sometimes even the birth experience itself is relived which is why the technique is popularly known as Re-birthing.

How it can help

Revealing breathing is an ancient technique that reveals the hidden worlds of the human mind and is one of the quickest methods to circumnavigate the devastating effects of stress on an individual, releasing them from a lifetime of learned negative responses. David has been practising shamanism and healing for over 30 years. The metaphysics behind our own lives and the objects of our desires are always entwined within the law of our Karmic paths. There is no exception. Always, a change of our own inner energies is necessary for that which is desired and ourselves to synchronize and thereby manifest. This is the work of Re-birthing and one simple fact that true spiritual work and development is a non-local event and affects the whole field of humanity.

What happens during a session?

You breathe! It's that simple. You're in control the whole time and, with David's guidance, you breathe into your experiences, thoughts and feelings that lay dormant in your subconscious. You'll simply relax into your own mind and describe what you are seeing, thinking and feeling. David will help you the entire way through and make sure you are comfortable and relaxed. After the session, David will help you understand your experiences and answer questions.

I flew from Glasgow to London on the morning of the 15th January and then took the underground out to Camden where we had arranged to meet at midday. I got to the underground a little early and, to be honest, I was a bit nervous about what was going to happen but excited about the prospect of what I might learn about myself. I had done my usual research into the subject and read that some people had experienced what were described as past lives experiences and were able to decipher themes and lessons about themselves that in turn helped them in this lifetime; all I knew was that I was going to trust the process and just see what came up.

Around 20 minutes later than planned, David sauntered up to the entrance where I could see him. I knew what he looked like as I'd seen pictures of him on the internet, but he didn't know me from Adam, so I walked up and introduced myself. Now, David stands at just a little over 5 feet tall, is covered from top to bottom in tattoos and has hair all the way down to his butt; me, I stand at 6'3 with a shaved head and a big beard and look a bit like an unfit rugby player, so it was quite a picture to see the two of us standing there.

We walked back to David's flat in Camden. I wasn't sure what to expect of his place as I had in mind that he came from a showbiz family and in the 60s and 70s, his dad was one of the most famous performers in the UK, so I think I probably imagined something quite upmarket and grand, but perhaps that says more about me at that time.

It felt like it took no time at all to get to David's place as we were immersed in conversation from the minute we met. David led me into his small and humble two-bedroomed terraced flat which was neither flashy nor big, but from the moment I went inside, it felt very safe and homely. The first things I noticed on walking through the hallway were the amazing black and white pictures of David's father, Frankie Vaughan; his famous hat and cane were also sitting in the corner of the sitting room.

Before the process began, David talked me through the breathing exercise that would get me into the state required to enter into the revealing breathing work.

After only a few minutes of this, I was completely relaxed and on the verge of being unconscious, and what would unfold out of my subconscious narrative over the next few hours felt like I was only partly in control of what I was sharing.

The idea of this ancient therapy is that when you get to the relaxed state just before falling asleep, you are aware enough to be able to articulate your experience but relaxed enough not to be fearful, judgemental or question what stories come up.

The first few moments of this experience felt like I was about to take a quantum leap into another life. If you were brought up in the 80s, you may remember the Scott Bakula programme called Quantum Leap where the opening credits played a black and white movie reel, in fast speed, of hundreds of moments in time, including pictures of the first man on the moon, JFK, Marilyn Munro and Jimi Hendrix. Well, this is as close as I can get to describing my first chapter in this experience, except I wasn't going in fast forward, but more rewind and I wasn't seeing moments of world history but moments of my own history, then even moments and glimpses of what was later explained as possible past lives. Now, bear with me as we get further down the rabbit hole...

I am very aware that as soon as I mention the idea of past lives, that readers may fall into 3 categories; those who believe in past lives, those who don't and those who are open-minded. All three of these views are 100% fine by me. I can honestly say I went into this with an open mind not knowing what would come up, if anything, and all I am sharing here is my account of what happened. Remember, everything is just someone's story.

Over the next few hours, I stayed in this relaxed state with very little guidance from David once I was there. My role in this was just to share what I was seeing and hearing in my mind and David would note this down so that he could help me make sense of it later.

Some of the things that came up were memories of my childhood and others seemed to go further back. I later found out these were previous lives stories. There were vivid stories of being a soldier and fighting in the war, of being a prisoner of war, of being a doctor or healer of some sort in a concentration camp. As I went further and deeper into the state, other stories would unfold about lives as a college professor, a watchmaker and a traveller. What appeared to clearly show up out of this first session was that I have been here many times before. Have you ever wondered that yourself? Have you ever wondered if you've been here before? Or had a very intense déja vu or have you ever met someone for the first time and felt like you know them from a previous life? I have had this throughout my life, which was probably one of the reasons I was drawn to taking part in this session, and indeed, what drew me to reach out to David.

After coming out of the relaxed state and returning to "normal", David invited me into his kitchen and made a large pot of peppermint tea. We sat across from each other at his breakfast bar. I was still feeling very relaxed but felt that I had been through something that was both tiring and energising at the same time. As David sat across from me, I noticed he had a huge handful of handwritten notes. "How long was I under?" I asked, as if just coming round from a surgery.

"Around three hours," he replied.

As we went through the three hours of notes together, with David helping me make sense of the stories and how they were in many ways linked to each other, the whole process began to give me a profound understanding of why I do certain things and that some of these things would sometimes feel outwith my control. I began to see certain patterns of behaviour, some of which I thought I had picked up from my parents, but it now made more sense that these were repeating patterns of previous versions of me.

It was nearing 10 pm and I had now been with David for about 10 hours. I was exhausted from the session but excited at what had come up and that it actually made some kind of sense to me.

At the end of the session, David said to me that this would begin to make even more sense as the days and weeks went by and that I should be very aware of the universe sending me signs to help with this.

He asked me at the end of the session what I hoped I would get out of the time with him and taking part in the process.

I remember saying four things:

1. I wanted to know if there were things from my past that I needed to learn in order to be the best version of myself in this life.
2. I wanted to know what more I could do to heal the condition in my stomach.
3. I wanted to learn how to acknowledge the past and plan for the future but live in the present.
4. I wanted to find the strength and courage to hand in my notice and leave the charity I was with to start out on my own.

David asked that I keep a journal of things that happened in the coming weeks and months and suggested that we should get together in a few weeks' time to see how things were going. I left David's flat a little after 10:30 that evening and walked around Camden Town looking for somewhere that might still be open where I could get a drink and have something to eat as I hadn't eaten since breakfast. I found a little late-night Italian restaurant which was still open so went inside and asked for a table for one. I ordered a glass of red wine and some kind of pasta dish and the waiter said, "Have you been here before, sir?"

I inwardly laughed and said to myself, "Turns out I have been here many times before," but as I knew he was asking about his restaurant, I just smiled and answered no.

I sat in this quaint little back street Italian restaurant eating my pasta and drinking wine whilst flicking through my own notes from the session. I remember still feeling a little bit in a daze, but also with an immense feeling of relief and like someone had just given me the answers to some of the biggest questions I ever had and this, in turn, made me feel powerful beyond belief. I finished my food, paid the bill, tipped the waiter and slowly ambled through the streets of Camden back to the hotel where I was staying. That night, I slept more soundly than I had in years. I woke up feeling fresher than I could ever remember and slowly and mindfully packed my things and headed to London City Airport. The whole morning felt like it was on purpose; everything felt like it had a flow to it. If you've ever seen the movie 'Limitless', where Bradley Cooper takes a pill that allows him to access 100% of his brain and has periods of absolute clarity, then this is as close as it got for me. I got to the airport, through security, grabbed a coffee and went to the gate. The plane was on time and I used the 1-hour flight back to Glasgow to continue reading my notes and trying to make more sense of them.

Once I was back home and with my wife, she asked how my trip had been and how the session had gone. Even though I had written about 50 pages on the session since leaving David's the previous night, I was still finding it difficult to find the words to explain the experience and what had come up for me. My wife understood and just said to tell her more about it when I felt I could make sense of it and that she was happy that, in some way, I had got what I went for.

In the weeks and months following the session, I threw myself further into my meditation practice as this also helped me think more clearly about the revealing breathing session and would also allow me to process things in a bit more detail and make some connections to the themes that showed up in the different life stories that came up. I had regular check-ins with David which helped hugely with some of my questions, but there was one thing that I still needed to work on - finding the courage, strength and self-belief to make the move to leave my current role and go it alone.

As I looked back over my notes, which were growing day by day, I was starting to see overlap and similarities in the stories. There were themes emerging throughout all the chapters that showed that I was someone who thrived on seeing things through no matter what, and someone who had a reputation for getting things done and for taking risks for the greater good. Whilst there were chapters of overcoming adversity or facing huge challenges, the end result was always as a result of not giving in or giving up and taking leaps of faith for the sake of the greater good. I found some comfort in this and hoped that it might help me find the strength in this life to do what I needed to do to live to my potential.

The thing I was finding it hardest to do was to leave the job I was in. I was on a very good salary, I had given the place 10 hard years of my life, part of me still loved the work, but there was a toxicity to the place and an incongruence between what the place taught and what it actually practised. I could often feel the energy being sucked right out of me when I had to make decisions that didn't sit well with my own values. I remember saying to David that sometimes it feels like I say I am going to do one thing, but I am forced into doing the exact opposite. My exact words during one conversation were, "I feel like I am in a car and I indicate to go right and then, at the last minute, I decide to go left, which puts me and other people at risk."

David encouraged me to keep watching for signs that would help me know if I was going in the right direction and making the right choices.

About a week after this conversation, I received an email from the chairman of the charity I worked for. I was requested to meet with him and other board members, along with the CEO, the following Sunday out at our Loch Lomond venue. I was dreading telling my wife as I had already been working away for 2 weeks and had hardly seen her or our son and now, I had to tell her I would be away for yet another day at the weekend.

It felt like it was getting closer to me resigning and I think I was running out of excuses of why I should stay:

Maybe it will get better

Maybe you will get your mojo back

Maybe they won't ask you to do so much

Maybe Maybe Maybe…

Waiting for the right time to make any big decision rarely works.

Waiting for the inspiration to write this book didn't happen, I just started writing one day.

Waiting to lose weight before you start running rarely works, you just start running.

I was running out of excuses and had very much become like the whinging dog sitting on the nail. The only thing I was waiting for was more pain, and I didn't even know it at the time. But I was in full control of my destiny.

As that Sunday meeting grew closer, I had already decided it wasn't going to be a good day. My wife wasn't happy that I was going to it and said I should have just told them, no, but not wanting to rock the boat with the hierarchy, I had decided I should go. Before leaving that morning, I had been meditating and had put it out there to the universe to give me a sign that everything would be ok if I were to resign. I was looking for some sort of comfort to know that everything would be ok if I walked away from the job I was in.

I jumped in the car and started the hour-long journey to the meeting.

The destination required me to drive on a lot of back roads but I knew the road well and all the shortcuts. I had left in plenty of time as I wanted to get there early and make use of the great coffee machine I knew was there.

As I was driving along, I remember thinking about the patterns of stories of the revealing breathing sessions and thinking that I knew I had all this knowledge, all this evidence of my life's histories and answers to some of the questions that I had held for so long; I had a clear plan of what going out on my own would look like, I just had to find the courage to make that leap.

As I got to around 20 minutes away from the venue, a tractor pulled out in front of me almost making me swerve off the road. I kept my distance but was now stuck on a back road behind a tractor driving at 20 mph. I noticed the last three letters of the licence number of the tractor were MWB, my initials. I have a good memory for number plates of all the cars my dad ever had so, for some reason, I am drawn to them. A few minutes up the road, the tractor started to indicate left so I decided to indicate and overtake. Just as I approached and just as the tractor should have gone left, I was almost right up beside him and he then turned right! He almost pushed me right into the field he was going into. I blasted the horn and he gave me the middle finger which angered me even more as he had indicated one way and turned the other. (Can you see where this is going?) As I've mentioned, I am not one for believing in coincidence, so this very much felt like an obvious sign, between the license number, the fact that I had used the exact analogy of indicating one way and going another and asking for some obvious signs during my morning meditation.

I was now running a bit later than planned and was very aware that I didn't want to be late, or indeed, start without a nice coffee!

I was now 5 minutes from the venue, and, on the last stretch of road, I ended up stuck behind a 4x4 which was pulling a horsebox. At this rate, I was definitely going to

THE BEST OF YOU

be late. I could see the cut off up ahead and I noticed the indicator on the horsebox was signalling left. I hesitated to overtake given what had happened just a few miles ago, so I held back, and lo and behold, a few seconds later the 4x4 went right!

To me, this sign could not have been more obvious. We can read what we want into these situations, but for this to happen twice within just a few miles of each other and given the fact that I really didn't want to go to this meeting and thinking about all the reasons why I needed to move on, this was enough for me on that day. I pulled into the venue around 3 minutes before the meeting was about to start, grabbed a coffee from the machine and met the chairman in the hallway. I explained to him that I wasn't staying for the meeting and that I was exhausted, and they would not get anywhere near the best out of me, so I was heading home. He wasn't happy, to say the least, but I was done. I had experienced what I needed to and was given what I asked for, so off I went. I drove home quite slowly and was very reflective. I don't think I saw another car on the road on the way home; it was like someone had cleared the road just for me. I got home and my wife asked why I was home, and I told her what had happened. We spent the rest of the day in the garden with our son, drinking coffee and enjoying each other's company.

That night, I had another meditation and acknowledged the signs I had been sent, offered my thanks and made a promise that I would be ready and open to whatever was coming up.

It was only a few weeks after this day that I did indeed resign from the organisation and start out on my own. It still stands to be one of the best and most powerful decisions I ever made.

David Sye of Yogabeats has become a great friend over the years. He continues to work around the world, changing it one person at a time through his unique training programme and the spiritual presence he brings. David has also been a guest and partner on many Best of You Programmes over the years and this is always an amazing addition to the programme.

I feel I took a bit of a risk with this chapter. This is not something I would normally talk about on programmes, as it opens up lots of questions about reality, beliefs, past lives, religion, etc., but remember, we all have our own beliefs and things that we draw comfort from - it's what makes us unique. All I can tell you is that for me, meeting David and going through these sessions with him gave me strength and insight into a number of different versions of myself, gave me a greater understanding of my life's behaviours and patterns and ultimately, gave me the wisdom to act on the knowledge I held.

Now, deciding to take part in a revealing breathing session is not something to take lightly. It is also not easily accessible as there are literally only a handful of people in the UK that can facilitate such a therapy. I was lucky that I found David in the way that I did and at the time I did. And I am also not suggesting that you need to know how you lived your past lives in order to know what to change in this life. Often, we know exactly what it is that holds us back, it's just that we have created such a strong habit or belief around it that we feel it impossible to change. However, one thing I know for sure is that when we look inwards for the answers instead of towards other people, we often find more than we can imagine. This can be done through meditation, prayer, mindfulness or whatever allows you time and space to be still and alone with your own thoughts. Training the inner dialogue you have with yourself can indeed be the one thing that changes how you feel about yourself and how you choose to conduct your life. Becoming your own best friend and valuing yourself can bring an end to patterns of repeated self-sabotage and constant criticism.

10. Reflective questions for positive self-talk

Take a few moments to reflect on what it might be like if you changed how you viewed yourself. Imagine if most of your inner conversations were powerful, encouraging, even inspiring! Imagine if, when you needed picked up from a low mood, it was your inner voice that helped you and not someone else, or if the advice that you really needed to hear came from your own mind and not from someone who doesn't know the real depths of you.

- What might you say to yourself during times of challenge?
- What advice might you offer when you seek guidance on something?
- How might you comfort yourself during times of sadness or trauma?

CHAPTER 9

Everything is perspective

"If we change the way we look at things, the things we look at change"

~ Dr Wayne Dyer

Since my early teens and my diagnosis, I had viewed my condition of ulcerative colitis as a sort of curse, a chronic condition that had the potential to limit my lifestyle and affect my future; even though I had managed to keep it well under control for most of life, this was still how I viewed it. I remember going through long flare-ups which, at the time, could be quite debilitating and saying to myself, "If only I didn't have this condition, my life would be so much better," or "I promise, if this condition goes away, I will never ask for anything again in my life."

It wasn't until I was in my early 30s and when I met David Sye and went through the sessions with him that one day he said, "You know, I didn't actually cure myself of colitis, Mark, I just changed the way I looked at it, I stopped seeing it as such a burden and sure I made some big changes to my lifestyle through Yoga and meditation and all that, but it all boils down to how you look at things."

This took me a while to get my head around but when I really thought about the condition and what it had taught me about myself over the years, regarding how to look after myself, the importance of a healthy mind as well as a healthy body, the need to experience silence and stillness where possible and the importance of slowing down, these were all things that helped look after the condition. That is, as well as having an incredible wife who looks after me very well, cooks from scratch for almost every meal and doesn't let me get caught up in negativity.

I started to look at my condition as a sort of barometer of how I was doing in life. When I was looking after all aspects of myself, my emotional, physical, mental and spiritual health and not overdoing it with work, stress, worry, eating, drinking, etc., and living a life that was in line with my values on how to treat people and what to put out into the world, then my health always seemed to be in top condition. Yet, if I let things slip and started to take on too much work, which would add to stress which I would worry about, then binge eat and over-drink at the weekend, then I would fairly quickly become symptomatic and would react to this with further worry and then the whole cycle began again. So, I started to look on the condition as a sort of internal checker and I told myself that I was lucky to have such a gift - many people don't have an internal checker to let them know that their insides are only responding to how you're treating them on the outside, and that it will give you a warning if you are not treating yourself right; other people, who are not so lucky, don't often get the warnings and by then it's too late.

I have used this strategy and the others that I have mentioned in this book for many years and still to this day remain healthy, with no surgeries and only the occasional low-level flare-up which I don't overreact to and just deal with it on the rare occasion it shows up. And as I said, there is usually a reason it shows up; it's trying to tell me something and all I need to do is listen.

This strategy is something that I use in other areas of my life and share during programmes, where people can sometimes get stuck in the mode of blaming their situation or their past for the suffering they are going through in the present.

I was running a programme for a charity in Glasgow called Bridging the Gap - they are known throughout Scotland for their inspirational and innovative work with young people and their families - their transitions work for young people entering into high school and they are well-known for their tremendous work around tackling sectarianism.

Bridging the Gap has been a partner of the Best of You Programme since the beginning back in 2010 and continue to use the programme to this day.

A few years ago, I was running a programme for them in the Gorbals for a group of high school students who were also going to be volunteers for Bridging the Gap. Most of the young people were from working-class families and were doing well at school. They were attending the programme to help with confidence and motivation as they moved on to the next chapter in their life. One lad on the programme didn't fit into the same category as this as he was living in a local authority care home and had been rejected by his parents due to him choosing to change his gender identity. The lad showed up for every single session and gave it everything, he stepped up to all the challenges and spoke out when he could and was such an important part of the group dynamic. One evening, when we were having a conversation about ethics and morals, he shared that although he didn't like living in care, it wasn't an entirely bad thing. He said that he could've allowed his parents to change his mind and live the rest of his life being someone that he wasn't and would not need to live a lie for the rest of his life, or he could live the life that he believed he was born to live. He used this line and it has stuck with me ever since.

"You can't control what hand you're dealt in life, but you can control which cards to play, and you can also shuffle them in any order you wish."

I found this incredibly insightful and inspiring for a 15-year-old who had been through all that he had and to look at his situation a little differently with a positive tone instead of one of blame and bitterness. It is young people like this who give me the inspiration and fuel to continue running the programmes and doing what I do.

It's a well-known and sometimes clichéd saying that "Perspective is everything". This, for me, is better translated in the opening quote of this chapter by the legendary Dr Wayne Dyer:

"If we change the way we look at things, the things we look at change."

Over the years, I have read hundreds of biographies of well-known celebs and world influencers who have come to a recognition through their ability to see things differently, and turned their often-challenging circumstances into ones of inspirations and victory. Most of us love a good underdog story. I have been attracted to this type of story since the early 80s when I first witnessed Rocky Balboa go from deadbeat debt collector to world champion. Although a story based on fiction, it was loosely based on the real-life story of Rocky Marciano's rise to victory from humble beginnings.

I remember years later reading how Walt Disney was bankrupt and all but homeless, but he knew inside that his little friend and alter ego, Mickey, would eventually be recognised and that he just needed to keep the faith and see his situation as a chapter that would further strengthen his belief in his vision. I also remember being inspired on hearing the story of Colonel Sanders, the visionary behind KFC, the world's first franchised restaurant chain. Colonel Sanders faced adversity from very early on when he lost his father when he was only five. He then became a father himself in his late teens; his wife later left him and took their daughter, then he spent some time in the army and ultimately ended up washing dishes in a small café. It wasn't until he was 65 that he had the idea of selling his famous fried chicken from the café he worked in and this later became the biggest food franchise of its time.

To this day, I still enjoy reading stories and watching movies about those who have weathered tough and challenging times only to turn their story into their greatest asset. I witness this in real life almost every week with those who take part in my programmes and I also use my own story as a catalyst and a window to allow others to begin viewing their own story as one of power and strength and not getting stuck in the darkness of victimhood.

I often use movie therapy on various programmes, as this can allow participants to connect to characters or plot lines that they may feel they recognise in themselves or, indeed, they can relate to. As a huge movie fan myself, there are so many characters that I have been able to identify with over the years and stories that I have been able to relate to through my own challenges that I have weathered.

One thing that I respectfully ask of participants, once they have graduated from the programme, is that where and when possible, they can in some way pay their experience forward. So, if they meet someone who is struggling with their confidence, self-belief, or lack of motivation or whatever it may be, they have to share their experience with them, help them or even help raise their awareness to what might be possible for them if they put in the work.

Social media is often full of stories of random acts of kindness and of people helping others who sometimes they have never even met.

Many years ago, I watched the movie 'Pay it Forward' starring Kevin Spacey and Hayley Joel Osmont (that's right, the wee guy from 'The Sixth Sense' that saw dead people.)

Anyway, in this movie in the opening scene, it's Trevor's (Hayley Joel) first day of the 7th grade and on day one, he meets his new teacher, Mr Simonet (played by Kevin Spacey). Mr Simonet asks his class the question, "What does the world expect of you?" Trevor answers, "Nothing, we are 11."

The conversation goes on between the teacher and his pupils but ends in a powerful monologue from Spacey:

Now...
...this <u>class</u> is <u>social</u> studies.
That is, you and the world. Yes.
There is a <u>world</u> out <u>there</u> and even if
you don't want to meet it...
...it's <u>still</u> <u>going</u> to hit you

right in the face.

Believe me.

Best <u>start</u> <u>thinking</u> <u>about</u> the world
now and what it <u>means</u> to you.

What does the <u>world</u> mean to you?

Come on! A <u>little</u> class
participation.

Is it just this <u>class</u> you
want to get out of?

Your house, your street?

Any <u>further</u> any of you want to go
than that? Yes?

The mall. That's only two miles
away from me.

Let me ask you <u>another</u> question.

How <u>often</u> do you <u>think</u> <u>about</u> things
that <u>happen</u> <u>outside</u> of this town?

Do you <u>watch</u> the news? Yes? No?

All right, so we're not <u>global</u> thinkers
yet, but why aren't we?

Because we're 11.

Good point. What's your name?

Trevor.

Maybe Trevor's right. Why should
we <u>think</u> <u>about</u> the world?

After all, what does the world
expect of us?
Expect?
Of you.
What does the <u>world</u> <u>expect</u> of you?
Nothing.
Nothing.
My God, boys and girls, he's right.
Nothing.
Here you are. You can't drive.
You can't vote.
You can't go to the bathroom
without a pass. You're stuck...
... <u>right</u> here in the <u>seventh</u> grade.
But not forever...
... <u>because</u> one day you›ll be free.
But what if on that day you' re free...
...you haven't prepared,
you' re not ready...
...and yet you look <u>around</u> you
and you don't like what the <u>world</u> is.
What if the world...
...is just a big disappointment?
We're screwed.
Unless....

Unless you take the <u>things</u> that you
don't like <u>about</u> this world...
...and you flip them <u>upside</u> down right
on <u>their</u> ass.
Don't tell your <u>parents</u> I
used that word.
And you can <u>start</u> that...
...today.
This is your assignment.
Extra credit.
It goes on all year long.
Wait a minute.
What's <u>wrong</u> with this?
What's the matter? Yes?
It's, Like, so....
There must be a word to finish
that sentence.
-Someone help her.
-Weird.
Weird. Crazy.
Hard.
-Bummer.
-Bummer.
Hard.
How <u>about</u> possible?

Written on the board is this year-long assignment in these words.

'Think of an idea to change the world
and put it into action.'

Trevor is the only one who really pays attention to this and takes it literally, that his job is indeed to start something now that will make the world a better place by the time he graduates.

Trevor is an 11-year-old who is being raised by his single mum who holds down two jobs and has a drink problem. He spends a lot of his time on his own and often has to cook his own meals and get himself out to school.

This is a character that many of the young people on my programmes can relate to.

Trevor comes up with a plan of how to change the world through random acts of kindness and draws up a plan of how this is going to work.

YOU

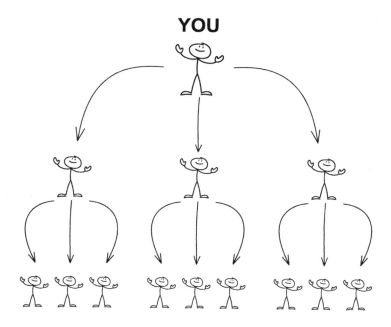

The idea is that you have to help three people by doing something for them that they cannot do for themselves and this isn't a favour where you ask for something in return. Instead, you ask them that when they can, they also do something for three other people and pay the good deed forward, and so on and so on. But it is really important that you pay it forward to at least three people so that the chain doesn't break through complacency.

As the movie unfolds, Trevor helps his three people with things that they cannot do for themselves - this includes feeding a homeless man, helping his mum find love with the right person and saving his friend from a beating. In case you decide to watch this movie, I won't spoil the ending, except to say to have the tissues at the ready.

But without giving too much away, throughout the movie you see what happens when people start to offer these random acts of kindness and look for nothing back, only paying forward to three people and then those three turn it into nine and …. You get the picture. But in the end, you see that it has become a movement and is infinite because so many people are now doing it. It's an incredible movie and has a powerful message that this inspirational movement started with an 11-year-old, who had plenty of reasons to moan and complain about his life, deciding to take the class assignment seriously, put it into action and try and make the world a little bit better.

I have met and worked with so many inspirational and strong young people like Trevor who have an incredible amount of creativity and resilience despite their often-chaotic life circumstances and family backgrounds. It never ceases to amaze me just how young people can adapt to their situation and just get on with it, treating it as their norm. On the other hand, we also have those who are known as "The Snowflake generation".

This is a disparaging term <u>now commonly used to refer to young people</u>, who are perceived to be over-sensitive and intolerant of disagreement. They live in the blame culture, are easily offended (often on behalf of other people) and have a strong sense of self-entitlement. Now, this may seem harsh and contradictory to some of the topics I have shared in this book, but it would be remiss of me not to say a little bit about this. If you think about it, you probably know who I am talking about. Most of us have one or more of them in our family. I know I have one in particular who has an opinion on everything, gets offended if you gently challenge this in any way, doesn't have a nice word to say about anyone or anything, gets offended easily, especially on behalf of other people and blames everyone else if things go even a little wrong. Now, I am not saying that there is anything actually wrong with this. Most parents of young people like this just label it as their age, or a phase, or it's the terrible teens, and that's ok to a point, but some of these attitudes and behaviours do need to be guided and, at times, challenged, as it's when this attitude travels into adulthood and becomes their norm that trouble can come looking for them, and then there is no one to blame.

When I think of Trevor and his passion behind Pay It Forward and the thousands of young people and adults that I've had on my programmes over the years who continue to overcome their adversities and go on to achieve and do amazing things in their lives, it gives me a huge sense of hope and optimism for the future.

As I have mentioned, this book is being written right smack bang in the middle of the Covid-19 pandemic and the country is still on lockdown; well, those of us who are still sticking to the rules are on lockdown!

But when this happened, we all had a choice to make of how we were going to respond and how we were going to view the situation.

Many people went into complete blind panic when the world went into lockdown. This was 100% acceptable as there is no one alive in the world who has been through a situation like this before. Some decided to take it day by day, follow the rules and just try and do their bit to keep the infection rate down by staying at home; again, 100 % acceptable. Some businesses and entrepreneurs went into overdrive and started designing online products and services and taking advantage of having a more captive audience and also trying to offer their services online; also acceptable. You then had the greedy ones and the selfish ones like Tim Martin of the famous pub and restaurant chain Wetherspoons, who sacked all 43000 of his staff and told them they could get jobs at Tesco during the pandemic; this, for me, was not acceptable.

I have also mentioned in previous chapters that I am not a naturally calm person or one who doesn't overreact at times. I need to work at it on a daily basis by raising my awareness of it and applying what I know works. So, when lockdown was announced and the pandemic hit, I had to sit back and think about my response. I knew I was going to be in a position of many things being outwith my control for some time, I knew I was going to have a lot of time on my hands, which is something I have not had for a very long time and I knew I was not going to be able to help and have the reach that I normally have for those that require support and guidance through my programme. So, after a few days of thinking, reflecting, planning and accepting, I wrote down these four things on headed paper.

March 2020

By the end of lockdown, here's what I will have achieved:

1. The first draft of the Best of You book will be complete
2. My 5k runs will average about 35 minutes (currently 40 minutes)
3. A full rebrand of Mark Brown Programmes Ltd will be complete
4. A redesign of all programmes to suit current needs

At the time of writing these very words, the date is the 23rd of June, we have been in lockdown now for over 12 weeks and restrictions have only just started to ease a little but are still very much in place to help tackle the infection rate.

Here's where I am at with my list:

1. I think I am about 2 chapters away from completing the first draft of the book
2. My 5k time is down to 37 minutes

3. My rebrand is now sitting with an agency and will be complete in a few weeks

4. The programmes are almost completely revamped and up to date with what I feel will be of great use going forward.

I chose my response to be one of service to three areas: a) to myself in regards to my mental and physical health, as I know when I run, I feel healthy and much more energetic, b) to other people in regards to finishing the book and hoping the book will be of great help to those that need it and want to do something about it, and c) to my company; I don't take it lightly or for granted how sought-after my programmes are. Whilst I am very lucky to have loyal partners and almost 100% returning business, I make it a priority to ensure that each programme is delivered to the absolute best of my ability each week and that every single person taking part feels valued, respected, motivated and ready to take action on the next chapter of their life. That is my 'pay it forward', when they use what they learn for themselves and others, and hopefully, this little corner of the world will be a better place for it.

Reflecting on this last chapter and as we near the final chapters in this book, I would like you to think about what you have yet to offer this world.

Allow yourself some time to think about these questions and write down your answers.

But do NOT write down anything that you are not willing to take action on.

11. Questions for action

- What have I yet to offer the world?
- What would it look like?
- What would it feel like?
- What would be different for me?
- What would I notice?
- What would others notice?
- What impact would it have?
- What would be different one year from now if I were to start doing this today?
- Can I do this?

CHAPTER 10

The power of intention

*"Twenty years from now, you will be more dis-
appointed by the things you didn't do
than by the ones you did do. So, throw off
the bowlines. Sail away from the safe harbour.
Catch the trade winds in your sails.
Explore. Dream. Discover."*

~ Mark Twain

Something that I wanted to avoid when writing this book was to offer a '12-step process, 6 steps to success, a power of 4, the magic of 8, or the science of 10' kind of read. Don't get me wrong, I have probably read all the above and taken something from it in some way or other and I am by no means telling you not to read these types of books. However, I wanted to offer something more personal about the work that I do every day, the people I have had the pleasure of meeting and working with along the way and who have in some way changed or shaped my life, and along with that, offer some hopefully useful skills and tools that will allow you to explore and uncover the Best of You.

Throughout the book, I have shared my thoughts and stories about the importance of curiosity, and how to be curious about your own potential. I've shared stories and thoughts about moving from victimhood to hero and the mindset that can help with this. I've highlighted the importance of the choices we make and just how much control we actually have over this.

I have talked about worry and ways in which to manage this better and the importance of spending some time on our own, thinking about how we see ourselves and what we hope people say about us through our actions and what we offer.

I have spoken about some of the mentors and key people who have influenced and, in many ways, shaped my life and helped me just get on with it and stop complaining about the past; they have also shown me the importance of acknowledging the past as our greatest teacher. And finally, I shared the importance of looking at things differently because when you do, the things you look at change.

I would like to finish with what I believe are the two most powerful and important practices that I know are life-changing when realised and have been key to the transitions I have made in my own life and continue to use in my own personal journey.

These are the power of intention and the power of manifestation.

I have touched on both of these throughout the book; it is impossible not to as they are inherent in all that I do.

I want you to think about why you bought this book in the first place - there would have been an intention there, so what was it?

. Sometimes, people buy books because they know the author and occasionally, people buy books just to look good on their shelves, but for the most part, people buy books to read them. Indeed, with books like this, people often read them as they want to make a change in their life or they are going through a transition in some way.

I believe nothing good or bad ever happened in this world without intention. Sometimes, we don't know consciously what the intention is but there is always an intention. When we realise this and grow our awareness of it, it can have a huge impact and influence over our decision-making process.

If you have read all of this book to this point, what have you done so far? Have you taken the time to think about the questions at the end of some of the chapters? Done some of the challenges? Or written down some notes? If you have, then great. You will already be noticing and practising some things differently and will be noticing change, particularly in your mindset and inner thinking. If you haven't done any of the questions, notes or challenges, then don't give yourself a hard time, just go back to your intention, think about why you bought this book and what you wanted to get out of it. If you have read it and not done the work, a lot of things will still have been taken in at a subconscious level, as it's almost impossible to read something and not take in at least some of it. However, if you are now thinking 'I wish I had done all of this as I think I would really get something out of it', then just go back to the end of each chapter and take the time to do the work. You have nothing to lose and everything to gain.

One thing we often do as human beings is to overwhelm ourselves with to-do lists, goals, targets, numbers, etc. I used to fall into this category but had a strong intention that I wanted to come away from this in order to A. live life more in the moment, and B. not live my life by the need to get to the end of a task list. Sure, I enjoy being productive and getting things done and having an overall sense of achievement, there's nothing wrong with that at all, but when you start to value yourself or others based on what they get done and how busy they are instead of valuing them for just being themselves or indeed yourself, you can get caught up on either living to get stuff done or being disappointed by what's not getting done.

My one and only rule for this is three words - "Keep it simple".

In fact, if there was one overriding message that I would hope came from this book, it would be just that - "Keep it Simple"; do the work, but "Keep it simple".

As a species, we are very good at both overcomplicating and overthinking things. We can do this by taking on too much and biting off more than we can chew or taking the simple things, overthinking them and adding to our already full plate.

If you're a fan of self-help and personal development books, you may have read the '7 Habits of Highly Effective People' by Stephen Covey. This book continues to be a best-seller for the simple reason that it ignores trends and pop psychology and focuses on timeless principles of fairness, integrity, honesty, and human dignity.

One of the greatest things I took from this book was Covey's explanation of doing things in a certain order to ensure productivity, managing your goals and living a balanced life. He has a great little visual exercise for this where he has one large bowl, a selection of small and large rocks, some sand and a couple of bottles of beer.

He usually asks people on his programmes to try and fit all the things into the bowl. When you see the exercise set up, it looks impossible to fit all that is there into the bowl, and you can see all the participants trying to be creative and trying many different ways to fill the bowl. Some start with the sand and try to bury the small stones in it, then add the big rocks at the top; others would pour the beer in, then the big rocks and then some sand. After around 20 minutes, the challenge comes to an end and Mr Covey then shares his philosophy of why doing the big rocks first is a great metaphor for life. He starts with putting the big rocks in first; he describes these as your priorities, the things that need to get done. He then adds in the smaller stones which begin to fill some of the gaps; these are the things that you don't always get done but really should. By this time, the bowl is almost full and visually, when you see it, you are thinking there is no way the sand and bottles of beer are going to fit in there. But, taking his time and very slowly, he begins to pour the sand over the stones and the rocks and you notice the sand filling every tiny little gap left and indeed, the sand goes all the way to the bottom and pretty much fills the bowl. These are the daily things that we never really get around to due to our overwhelming list. Then finally, just as you are thinking there is no way 2 bottles of beer are going to fit in this bowl as it now looks like it's at capacity, he takes the bottle tops off and begins to pour both bottles slowly into the bowl, and when you look closely, you can see the beer sinking into the sand and filling the tiniest of gaps between the grains of sand and the last drop takes it all right up to the brim. Often, someone will ask Mr Covey what the beer represents, and he will quip back, "No matter how busy you are, there should always be time for a couple of beers with friends".

The week before I quit my job, I was out for the day with my wife and two young kids. The kids were only 1 and 4 at the time and my weekends were precious as I was, at that time, working away a lot. We had gone to the beach for the day with a picnic as it was a rare sunny day in Scotland!

We had set everything out for our picnic and my son and I went to the water's edge to skim stones. Every so often, he would hand me a perfectly flat and round one that would get at least 10 jumps along the water surface. We went back to the picnic spot and Joshua had brought back a pile of stones to play with while we were eating.

I watched him for several minutes trying to build the stones into a little tower, but he couldn't get the last few on as it kept toppling over. Joshua is not someone to give up easily, nor does he get frustrated with this type of thing; he usually just tries different strategies until he finds what works. After about 10 minutes playing with the stones, he said, "Look, Daddy, I've done it! All 10 rocks on top of each other - you just need to put the big ones down first, see, then you can get the rest on top!"

Now, whether you believe it or not, and I certainly do, I strongly feel that the universe sends you signs in the strangest of ways, and Joshua and his rock tower on the beach was exactly that for me. I had already decided that I would soon be moving on, but I was already overthinking the process, overwhelming myself and starting to build a story of "what ifs".

In that moment, I chose to stay at the bottom of the ladder and remind myself that I knew putting the big rocks first and doing what needs done would allow me the time and space for all the other stuff. It's not a complicated strategy, you just have to use your common sense and realise that by getting the really big things on the list done, not only makes you feel good with a sense of achievement but gives a bit more energy and belief that the rest of your list is actually doable.

One thing that is really clear for me and helps me get things done, time and time again, especially the big things, is to be clear on what the intentions are for the big things.

I mentioned earlier that at the beginning of lockdown I wrote a list of things I would aim to achieve before the end of lockdown, not really knowing how long that would actually be.

The two biggest things on the list were also the ones I knew would take the longest: A. Writing the book and B. Improving my 5k running time. The first thing to be clear on is that both these things are 100 % possible. The only things getting in the way of them becoming a reality are me, my mindset and my intention. So, to begin with, I knew writing the book couldn't just be because I said ages ago, "Oh, I am going to write a book", and "Man, 45 mins for a 5k is pretty shit. I really need to do better".

No, I had to be really clear on the intention for both as they were the biggest things on the list and I knew that if I could achieve them, then others would fall into place like the grains of sand in the bowl.

So, when I wrote it down, it looked a bit like this:

Task – Write the Best of You Book
Intention – Write a book about your work that will reach even more people than the programmes currently do. Capture the essence of the programme so that those who may not be able to access a programme can learn the skills and tools shared on a Best of You.

Task – Get 5k daily runs under 35 minutes
Intention – Practice running every day to ensure stamina and energy levels get stronger; you know you always feel better when you are running most days. This will also give you the energy and mindpower to deliver your programmes to the highest standard.

By being crystal clear on the intention of what you are trying to achieve and knowing the wider impact of this, it will have a huge influence over how much energy and time you give to making it happen.

It also doesn't need to be something that you overthink or spend huge amounts of time on. As I said earlier, "Keep it simple".

When you are clear on what it is you want to achieve, just ask yourself why this is important and what impact will it have; be fairly instinctive as your gut will usually be right.

This book was written and designed to help you help yourself. It encourages you to look inward for inspiration, as that is usually where you find it for real. At no point in this book does it ask you to go and ask other people for advice or for their opinion. There is nothing to stop you asking other people for help or what they would do in the situation, and yes, at times, it is absolutely right to ask for help and support if you start to feel like you are on your own and that you need some outside help. However, know that you have strength and ability beyond what you thought was possible. If you are reading this book then it means you have survived every single challenge and curveball so far that life has thrown at you, and this book is just another string to your bow and tool in the box to help you take on the next chapters. Just remember, it's your story - you are the author, and you decide what's next for you.

11. Questions for your intentions

- Think about and write down between 5 and 10 things that you really want to get done, achieve, change, or start doing.

- For each of these things, write underneath them what the intention behind this is and ask yourself, what will this get me and what will the impact be?
- Sit back with your eyes closed for as long as you need to and really immerse yourself in what this journey is going to be like. Think about what it will be like a year from now if you start today with these powerful intentions in mind. Think about the impact this will have on you and those around you. Ask yourself what you will notice and what it will be like once these intentions come to fruition.

I am going to suggest that whatever you have written down for the above questions, you keep in your wallet or purse, or just somewhere where you can access it really easily, and just give yourself a daily reminder of why you are doing what you are doing and what the intention is behind it. This is where the power of manifestation comes in.

I mentioned this earlier in the book and shared Einstein's quote:

"Imagination is everything, it's the preview of life's coming attractions"

This, for me, is where the little bit of magic lies in turning our dreams, goals and aspirations into reality.

When we really give our intentions regular thinking time and space, we create an energy for whatever that thing is. And by thinking about these things daily and creating a clearer picture in our minds every time, that energy becomes stronger. And we know that once energy has a certain momentum and power behind it, it then becomes impossible to stop. So, how much thinking time and how much energy you give to your dreams and aspirations will directly impact how much momentum is created and ultimately how close you get to making them happen. Taking tiny but continuous steps is how momentum is created, but also, don't give yourself a hard time if you fall at a hurdle; remember, you've got up from every hurdle you've struggled with so far, otherwise you wouldn't be reading this book!

To really lock this last piece in, I am going to ask you to write a letter to your future self. I know, it may feel a little weird, but when you open this letter in a few months or a year from now and you have realised your potential and are living a different life due to what you yourself have manifested, only then will you begin to see the absolute power that you have over your life and which direction it takes and the impact you want to have. Once you realise this power, it will be like going to the gym to really build those muscles after noticing a little bit of definition. You will want more, you will manifest more, you will live more, and you will be more. Remember, this book is just the preview of coming attractions - you choose what you imagine, it's your mind, your story and you are the author.

Here's the letter I wrote to myself the year before I started my business:

Dear Mark

I hope you are well, and life is where you planned it.

If you are doing what you intended to and have manifested your thoughts, hopes and plans, then by this stage, you should have changed the 3 things below.

- Task – Leave your current job
  Intention – Start something that you have full autonomy over, will have a bigger impact on society, will require less time working away and will allow more time with family.
- Task – Keep stress levels to a minimum
  Intention – By leaving your current role in management, you will now only be responsible

for you, your decisions and your impact. You will have more control over your time, your health and your wealth.

- Task – Invest in yourself
  Intention – Invest time in yourself; keep up your meditation and mindful practices. This will keep you balanced and focused. Invest money in yourself. Go to all the training that you want to, do all that you can to keep growing and learning as a person.

I wrote this letter in January 2013, left it in a drawer in my office and put a reminder on my phone calendar to open and read it at the end of December the same year.

When I opened the letter and looked back over the year, I had left that job, created Mark Brown Programmes Ltd, had an almost full calendar for the following year, hadn't felt any relevant stress for most of that year, had done further training in meditation, reiki and coaching and would be travelling to Denmark the following year for further training. I have written a letter every year since.

When we get ideas out of our minds and onto paper, that is the first step of commitment. When we take that first step of taking action, it takes us just a little closer to making it happen, so, when we begin to repeatedly take action with a clear intention of why we are doing what we are doing, we create a habit, and when the habit sets in, change becomes inevitable. Once we make a conscious decision about what we want to focus on and are clear about the outcomes and the intention behind it, it just takes a little daily action to turn it into reality. We have been both subconsciously and consciously manifesting our realities and ambitions from the day we were born; it's just that as we get older, sometimes we forget we have this power.

Think about it. The two biggest skills and life-changing things we want to learn before we are 1 year old is walking and talking.

There is no magic wand for this whereby one day, we wake up and hey presto, we can do both. Nope, it is a process like every other dream and ambition we have. We see others do it, we see the benefits of it, we try hundreds of times, we fall many times, but that's the great thing about kids - when they fall, they don't sit there on their bums and say, "Right, that's it, walking isn't for me. I'll just spend the rest of my life down here". No, every single time they fall, they get back up, they find their balance and day by day, the habit gets stronger and stronger and before they know it, they don't even need to think about it. We are born to learn and create new habits, learn new skills, copy others and grow in the things we can do. This is the gift of being human. Our capabilities are only limited by our imagination, not the other way around. So, with this in mind, just take a moment to appreciate all that you have manifested and made happen in your life so far. We all started with walking and talking, we then started to feed ourselves and start forming opinions. We learned, manifested and developed hundreds of skills before we even started school. Then we learned reading, writing, subject matter, relationships, and the ups and downs of trying to fit in or stand out. You are an exceptional being with exceptional capabilities, so now is your time to become the best version of you. You are in the driving seat from now, so set your destination, and drive......

Afterword

It's an interesting feeling coming to the end of writing this book.

I started the book at the beginning of 2020 with an intro and a chapter or two, but I then struggled to find time to give it the attention it needed, so left it for a month or two. Then, Covid-19 happened, my full calendar of work and programmes was completely wiped, and lockdown was imposed on the entire nation.

Like many, I was faced with choices. I had the choice of panicking – in my experience it doesn't feel great and never solves anything – worrying – again, it doesn't feel great and rarely solves anything, or doing something productive - always feels good, can lead to great things, and then fills the gap making worry and panic hard to do.

So, on the 20th March, I wrote my list, set out my intentions, opened the laptop, told some stories, shared some insights and today, the 1ˢᵗ of July, here I am writing the afterword.

Now, I have choices regarding my mindset on what happens next.

I can have the "What's for ye won't go by ye" attitude - this was a quote in my family throughout my childhood, one that I don't actually care for too much, as I don't believe for a minute our lives are mapped out in such a way that we can't massively influence it by the actions we take. So, I won't use that option, I am just aware that it is one.

I could also decide to send this to a number of publishers in the hope that it is recognised as having some relevance in today's world. This is a very viable option.

I could invest myself and self-publish the book to ensure that it is printed, out there and available on the open market, also a viable option.

All I know at this stage is that my intention was to write something that would help people, reach those that it needed to and hopefully, in some way, inspire people to start exploring their own unique potential. Whichever option I choose, I know it will be the right one, and no matter what happens, this book will be out and available before the end of 2021. How do I know? Because you're reading it right now.

I hope to see you on one of my programmes somewhere along your journey. Until then, enjoy exploring the magic that is the Best of You.

Acknowledgments

The Best of You Programme continues to grow and be sought after throughout Scotland. There are many people I need to thank for their continued support that allows the programme to have the impact it has and who have helped this book come to life.

Firstly, a huge thank you to Lorna Walker, founder of Compassionate System. Your support and feedback during the process of writing this book has been hugely appreciated, and your input and time on the Best of You Programmes helps enhance the experience every time.

Craig Mathieson of the Polar Academy. You have been part of the Best of You experience since the very beginning and helped some of the most challenging and vulnerable young people believe that they are capable of so much more.

David Sye! Man, what a time we have had. Thank you for helping me shift my perspective on many things, for helping me delve into a spiritual realm that I never knew existed and thank you for what we have yet to achieve together.

Marie Laidig. Thank you for your support, your friendship, your counsel, your input into the programmes over the years and most of all, for supporting me many years ago to make the decision that finds me at the helm of The Best of You Programme.

Gordon Findlay. Your support and feedback throughout writing the book is hugely appreciated. But your support throughout my life has been incredible; from both moral and financial support back in the day when I quit my job to go back to college, to helping me almost land that big f**king fish that got away in Aberfoyle.

Barry "Boz" Brown. You raise your own bar time after time and inspire me to do the same. I know you look up to me too, but that's just a height thing. LYM

Mum and Dad. Thank you for everything! But, in particular, for bringing me up in a way that allowed me the freedom to be who I was meant to be, for instilling a moral compass that shaped my passion for trying to leave people in a better place than I find them, and for your continued support in all that I strive for.

Laura. Partner in life, business, parenting and everything else. You make everything possible and believe in me even when I don't.

You are the brains behind the business and the heart behind the family and there is no one else I'd rather be on this journey with. Here's to the next chapters.....

Finally, to all the schools, services, projects, young people and adults who participate in the programmes and take on the Best of You challenge to begin exploring their own potential, you are the reason this book exists, so a heartfelt thankyou to each and every one of you.

Printed in Great Britain
by Amazon

86148437R00122